Numbers

Dwelling in God's Word

Numbers

God's Presence and Promise in the Wilderness:
A Fifty-Day Devotional

GRAHAM JOSEPH HILL

Eagna Publishing • Sydney, Australia

NUMBERS

God's Presence and Promise in the Wilderness: A Fifty-Day Devotional

The publisher cannot verify the accuracy or functionality of website URLs used in this book beyond the date of publication.

Published by: Eagna Publishing (Sydney, Australia)
eagnapublishing@icloud.com
Cover and interior design: Graham Joseph Hill
www.grahamjosephhill.com

paperback isbn: 978-1-7643311-5-9
ebook isbn: 978-1-7643311-6-6
version number 2025-11-11

NATIONAL LIBRARY OF AUSTRALIA

A catalogue record for this book is available from the National Library of Australia

Contents

Introduction

This devotional is part of a larger pilgrimage through Scripture, shepherded by Rev. Dr. Graham Joseph Hill, as he walks with readers from Genesis to Revelation. The Dwelling in God's Word series (both podcast and written reflections) invites you to discover how each book of the Bible speaks to the deep longings of the soul and the demands of our shared life in the world. It's not merely a reading plan; it's a sacred journey of formation and transformation. Here, the biblical narrative meets everyday discipleship in prayerful and practical ways.

The Book of Numbers shimmers with the mystery of God's presence in the wilderness. It's a book for those who walk through dry seasons, who feel the ache of waiting, who wonder if the promise still holds. Numbers begins not in the land of abundance but in the desert of formation, where a fragile people learn to live between deliverance and fulfillment, mercy and judgment, complaint and grace.

Here, tents rise around a moving Presence. Clouds guide by day; fire glows by night. In this strange and sacred landscape, God shapes wanderers into worshipers, complainers into a covenant community. Every journey, every setback, every miracle becomes a lesson in trust: a call to follow the Presence even when the path feels barren.

Numbers tells the story of a people learning that holiness isn't about perfection but about staying close to the One who leads. It's the slow, painful beauty of transformation in motion. Beneath every rebellion runs a deeper rhythm of grace: God refusing to abandon a beloved people, God still choosing to dwell among them.

From Sinai's camp to the threshold of promise, Numbers reveals that even in wilderness places, God is faithful, patient, and near. It invites us to keep walking when hope runs thin, to believe that the desert can become holy ground, and to discover that every wilderness is a place where Presence and Promise meet.

This devotional is rooted in the richness of the biblical text and nourished by careful theological reflection. It invites you to sit with Scripture: slowly, reverently, attentively. Each entry draws you deeper into Numbers, exposing overlooked treasures and summoning fresh faith. But this isn't just about knowing more. It's about living differently. As you journey through these pages, you'll be challenged to embrace justice, embody mercy, cultivate humility, and become a participant in the reconciling mission of God.

These reflections don't avoid hard questions or flatten the text into sentiment. They dare to wrestle. To pray. To imagine. And they call you to more than contemplation. They invite you to action: to live the lessons of Numbers in your neighborhood, your body, your workplace, your church.

As you immerse yourself in this devotional, may your theology deepen, your heart soften, and your hands be ready to serve. May these fifty days in Numbers stir something courageous in you: a longing to see and be seen by the living Christ.

How to Use This Devotional:

1. This book leads you through Numbers in fifty short devotions.

2. You're encouraged to pair this with the companion podcast: https://grahamjosephhill.com/devotions.

3. Each day, you're invited to:

a. Read the passage slowly, letting it read you.

b. Sit with the day's devotion and let its truths sink deep.

c. Pray, honestly and vulnerably, into the text.

d. Discern one concrete action in response.

Whether you read alone, with family, or within a community, this journey through Numbers will shape your heart and stretch your faith. Come ready to be changed.

Day 1: When God Calls the People by Name

Reading: Numbers 1:1–19

The book of Numbers opens with naming. In the wilderness of Sinai (after the giving of the law, before the long journey toward promise), God speaks to Moses in the tent of meeting. The people are counted, tribe by tribe, name by name. This census is no cold bureaucracy. It's not a spreadsheet of statistics. It's a spiritual act, a re-membering of a people once enslaved, now called to bear covenant identity in the world.

"Take a census," God says, "of all the congregation of Israel." This command is about belonging. This is a community shaped by memory and mission. To count them is to affirm that each life matters, that no one is lost in the wilderness of forgetfulness. Every name is a story, every family a testimony, every tribe a piece in God's work of redemption.

Still, there's tension here. Counting can sanctify, but it can also control. The difference lies in who is doing the counting and why. Pharaoh once counted the Hebrews to enslave them. God counts them to send them. Pharaoh tallied their bodies for brickmaking. God names their souls for vocation. What empire uses to measure worth, God reclaims as a declaration of dignity.

This moment invites us to examine how we count, name, and remember people in our own age. We live in societies obsessed with data and productivity, where metrics replace meaning, and people become demographics rather than neighbors. The census of God resists that. It reminds us that divine accounting always begins with presence and ends in purpose.

The wilderness census also signals readiness. This is a preparation for mission. Each tribe will take its place in the movement toward promise, forming a living body ordered around the presence of God. The tent of meeting stands at the center: not a palace or throne, but the dwelling of divine companionship. From that center, the people are arranged and sent. Order flows from intimacy, not domination.

In our spiritual lives, we too are invited to pause and take stock, not of possessions or successes, but of the deeper census of the heart. Who are we becoming in the wilderness? Where is God calling us to stand, serve, or move? The naming of the tribes is a reminder that the God who numbers stars and knows the sparrow's fall still calls each of us by name.

At the heart of this text stands a revelation: holiness is found in gathering, and vocation begins with being seen. To be counted by God is to be claimed for God's purpose.

And in Jesus, the census of grace expands. No tribe is left unnamed. No wanderer forgotten. The Shepherd who knows each sheep by name gathers a new people: numbered not for conquest but for compassion, not for war but for witness.

Guiding Truth: God's counting restores dignity: every name known, every life called, every story gathered for divine purpose.

Reflection: How does it change me to believe that God knows me by name, not by number or performance? Where might God be inviting me to help others feel seen, counted, and remembered?

Prayer: God of the wilderness and the tent, thank you for calling me by name. In a world that forgets, teach me to remember. Count me among those who serve your purposes, walk in your presence, and honor every life as precious in your sight. Amen.

Day 2: Ordered for Mission, Not for Domination

The census continues, tribe by tribe, name by name, number by number. It's a long and careful record of who stands ready for the journey. What might feel like dry accounting is, in truth, the architecture of vocation. God is shaping a people not for chaos, but for calling; not for conquest, but for covenant purpose.

Each tribe is named, counted, and placed within the community's greater order. But this order isn't hierarchy; it's harmony. The point isn't who's most powerful, but how the whole people can move together toward promise. The God of Israel isn't the god of empire; this isn't the arrangement of armies for domination, but the formation of a people for witness. The divine intention is always relational: structure serves love, not control.

Twelve tribes stand ready. They aren't perfect; they're often quarrelsome, fearful, and frail. Yet God still unites them into a body: imperfect yet chosen, flawed yet called. Their strength lies not in their numbers, but in their sense of belonging. What counts most isn't the headcount but the heart behind it.

Significantly, the Levites are excluded from the military census. They're not forgotten but set apart for a different kind of strength: the strength of worship, intercession, and sacred service. While others stand guard at the edges of the camp, the Levites guard the center, tending to the tabernacle: the holy dwelling where heaven touches earth. This reminds us that God's people are sustained not only by defense and strategy but by devotion and presence. Without the priests of prayer, the warriors lose their compass. Without the tent at the center, the camp becomes a mere army instead of a holy nation.

In today's world, we're tempted to measure worth by efficiency, visibility, or output. Yet the story of Numbers 1 offers another truth: every calling matters. Some are sent to lead, while others are sent to intercede. Some are stationed at the frontlines of public life, others in the humble shadows of worship or care. But all are vital in the unfolding of God's mission. Holiness isn't found in sameness: it's found in the symphony of distinct callings united by love.

Spiritually, this passage invites us to take stock of the order in our own lives. What is at the center? What holds the camp of our days together? When devotion drifts from the middle, even our best structures collapse into restlessness. But when God dwells at the center, even the wilderness becomes sacred ground.

This isn't a text about bureaucracy or boundaries. It's a vision of beloved order: a life oriented around divine presence, each person carrying the weight of calling, the wonder of being seen. It's a reminder that discipleship isn't random; it's deliberate, communal, grounded in God's presence and purpose.

And, as in all of Scripture, this story points forward: to Jesus, the new center of God's people. Around him, the weary find order, the lost find belonging, and the restless find home. The census ends where grace begins: one body, many members, moving in rhythm with love.

Guiding Truth: God's order is never about control; it's about communion; every calling finds meaning when centered on divine presence.

Reflection: What sits at the center of my life: fear, ambition, or the presence of God? How might I honor the diverse callings within the body of Christ more fully?

Prayer: God of presence and purpose, reorder my heart around you. Teach me to see every role in your kingdom as holy. Let my life, with others, move in harmony with your will, that your glory may dwell at the center of all I am. Amen.

Day 3: God at the Center

Reading: Numbers 2:1–34

In the wilderness, God teaches a scattered people how to live with holy order. The tribes of Israel are arranged around the tabernacle, not in random lines or competitive ranks, but in a sacred pattern. The tent of meeting rests at the heart of the camp, the dwelling place of divine presence. Everything radiates from there.

This arrangement is a form of liturgy. The camp's design is a living theology. At the center of Israel's identity is the presence of God. The tent stands where empire would put its palace. God dwells, not above or beyond, but among. Every movement of the people begins with this truth: the Holy One travels with them.

Each tribe takes its place, facing the tabernacle and oriented toward the divine center. Judah leads from the east: the direction of sunrise, symbol of new beginnings. The tribes are encamped as a body, each distinct yet united in purpose. The arrangement reminds them (and us) that faith isn't a private journey; it's a communal pilgrimage toward a shared center.

The Levites encircle the tabernacle, guardians of holy space. Their task is to tend what others might overlook: the rhythms of worship, the maintenance of the sacred, the remembrance of presence. Without them, the people might march efficiently but forget whom they follow. The Levites ensure that holiness remains the heartbeat of the journey.

In a world that worships autonomy, Numbers 2 is a rebellion. It insists that life finds meaning not when we stand at the center, but when

God does. We are constantly tempted to reorder the camp around our desires, our achievements, our fears. But spiritual health begins with reorientation: with letting the presence of God be the still point around which everything else turns.

When we lose that center, chaos begins to creep in. Our ambitions expand, our communities fracture, our faith thins into performance. But when we let the divine presence anchor us, everything else begins to fall into alignment. Work becomes a vocation. Rest becomes worship. The community becomes a reflection of divine order rather than a competition of human striving.

This chapter also reminds us that divine order celebrates diversity. Each tribe has its banner, its place, its task. The unity of Israel rests on harmony within difference. The Spirit of God still calls the church to embody that: one body, many parts, each facing toward the same Presence.

In Jesus Christ, this wilderness vision finds fulfillment. The Word becomes flesh and "tabernacles" among us. The divine center moves from tent to heart, from fabric to flesh. Christ becomes the Presence at the center of our lives and communities, calling us to live outward from grace rather than inward toward self.

The question isn't whether God is in the camp. The question is whether we've turned our tents toward the Presence.

Guiding Truth: True order begins when God (not ambition, fear, or ego) dwells at the center of our lives and communities.

Reflection: What has drifted into the center of my life that displaces divine presence? How might I help my community turn its tents toward God's presence again?

Prayer: God who dwells among us, be the still point of my life. Recenter my heart around your presence. Teach me to live in harmony with your people and your ways, that all my days might revolve around your glory. Amen.

Day 4: The Sacred Weight of Service

Reading: Numbers 3:1–39

In the wilderness, God does something remarkable: appoints a people to guard holiness. The Levites are set apart, not for privilege but for presence. Their calling is to serve and to protect the mystery the tabernacle holds.

The chapter opens with the lineage of Aaron and Moses: those who stand in the tension between divine holiness and human frailty. Then it moves outward, naming the clans of Levi: Gershon, Kohath, and Merari. Each clan is assigned a distinct task: tending to curtains, carrying sacred objects, and safeguarding the structure. This is hidden, repetitive, and weighty work. But in the economy of God, these acts sustain the holy center.

The Levites' service is an act of mediation. They stand between the people and the presence of God, ensuring that holiness doesn't consume and that indifference doesn't profane. Their vocation embodies reverence: an awareness that divine nearness is both gift and fire.

This passage teaches us something countercultural: that holiness needs caretakers. In a world obsessed with platform, visibility, and control, God honors those who guard the unseen spaces: the prayers in the night, the acts of mercy that never trend, the faithfulness that no one applauds. The Levites remind us that service is sacred precisely because it's hidden. The world sees hierarchy; God sees stewardship.

Each family of Levi knows its place and portion. Gershon's clan carries the curtains: the fabric that forms the dwelling. Kohath's family carries the ark, the lampstand, and the altars: symbols of divine glory. Merari's descendants bear the frames and bases: the very skeleton of the sanctuary. None can replace the other. If one neglects its call, the whole structure collapses. The body of God's people depends on the faithfulness of many hands.

The Levites camp close to the tabernacle, surrounding it like living walls. They're a protective circle of worship and vigilance. Their proximity to the presence is both an honor and a danger. They carry holy things, yet they mustn't touch or gaze upon them directly. Holiness is participation through obedience.

This text presses gently but firmly: what sacred trust has been placed in our care? Perhaps it's a community, a child, a calling, or a truth to guard with integrity. To follow Christ is to share in the Levites' vocation: to protect what's holy in a world that treats everything as disposable.

In the church, too, there are no small callings. Some teach, some heal, some clean, some intercede, some hold the fragile frame of the community together. All serve the same Presence.

And in Jesus, the pattern is fulfilled. He becomes the true High Priest: the One who carries not curtains or frames but humanity itself into the heart of God. In his life and death, the tabernacle moves from canvas to flesh. We aren't only invited to guard the holy, but also to become its dwelling.

Guiding Truth: Holiness is sustained by hidden faithfulness; the sacred weight of service rests on those who guard God's presence with humility and love.

Reflection: What "holy things" has God entrusted to my care that I might have taken for granted? How can I practice faithfulness in the hidden, unseen work of love and service?

Prayer: Holy One, teach me the reverence of the Levites. Let me carry the sacred weight of service with humility and joy. Guard my heart from pride, and make my life a dwelling place of your presence, sustained by faithfulness and love. Amen.

Day 5: Redeemed for the Holy Work of Love

Reading: Numbers 3:40–51

The counting continues, but this time, it carries a different tone. God tells Moses to number the firstborn males of Israel, from one month old and up. These firstborns, by ancient right, belong to God. They are symbols of deliverance, living reminders that on the night of liberation from Egypt, Israel's firstborn were spared. Each life testifies: we were rescued by mercy.

Yet here, God does something extraordinary. Instead of taking the firstborn into temple service, God appoints the Levites in their place. The Levites become living stand-ins, a substitution not of rejection, but of representation. They are given to God as an offering from all Israel, serving in the tabernacle as the embodiment of the people's collective devotion.

But what about those who outnumber the Levites? God instructs Moses to redeem the remaining firstborns with silver: five shekels each, the price of holy exchange. The people pay not to escape service but to affirm that all life is sacred, that every firstborn (and indeed, every person) belongs first to God. Redemption here is transformation. It marks the people as a community ransomed by grace and called to live accordingly.

This passage, at first glance, feels like arithmetic. Yet beneath the numbers beats the pulse of theology. The exchange between the firstborn and the Levite, between silver and service, reveals a deeper truth about divine ownership and mercy. Every life is held in God's claim, yet God's claim is never coercive. It's covenantal. To be "God's own" is to find one's true purpose.

In a world that prizes autonomy, this truth is radical. We imagine belonging as a limitation. Scripture insists it's liberation. To belong to God is to be freed from the tyranny of self, from the illusion that we are our own masters. It's to live as participants in God's redeeming work.

The ransom of the firstborn also echoes forward: to the cross, where the ultimate exchange takes place. The language of substitution finds its fulfillment in sacrifice, and not in the Levites but in Christ. He becomes the firstborn among many siblings, the priest who embodies our offering, the ransom that sets creation free. The temple becomes the heart; the redemption price becomes love.

For our spiritual lives, this text calls us to remember who we are and whose we are. Each of us has been "counted and redeemed" for participation in the holy work of love. Redemption is what God does for us, in us, and through us. The redeemed become redeemers, offering presence, compassion, and justice in a world that's forgotten its worth.

Numbers 3 ends not with bureaucracy but with blessing. Every name, every coin, every act of obedience testifies to a God who reclaims what's been enslaved and restores it to purpose.

Guiding Truth: To be redeemed is to be reclaimed for love: set free from self-possession to serve in the presence of God.

Reflection: What does it mean for me to belong wholly to God, not as property but as beloved participant in divine purpose? How might my daily life reflect the gratitude of one who has been ransomed by grace?

Prayer: Redeeming God, you have counted me, called me, and claimed me as your own. Teach me to live as one set free, not for myself but for love. Let every act of my life become a small offering of gratitude to your boundless mercy. Amen.

Day 6: The Weight of the Holy

Reading: Numbers 4:1–20

The wilderness is filled with movement: tents rising and falling, fires kindled and extinguished, a people following the pillar of cloud and flame. Yet amid this motion, there's deep care for the holy. Numbers 4 opens with instructions for the sons of Kohath, a family within the tribe of Levi, chosen to carry the most sacred objects of the tabernacle.

But they're warned: they mustn't touch the holy things or even look at them, or they'll die. Reverence is protection. Holiness, unmediated, is like fire: beautiful, consuming, alive. God's presence isn't something to be handled casually. The priests must first cover every sacred object with cloth and skin before the Kohathites approach. Only when the holy has been veiled may it be borne upon their shoulders.

The imagery is rich and trembling with meaning. The coverings preserve the mystery of divine nearness. The sacred is protected from triviality, and the people are protected from presumption. In a world that commodifies everything, this passage reminds us of the value of a sense of awe. There are still things too holy to be stripped bare, mysteries that must be carried with trembling hands.

The task of the Kohathites is both exhausting and dangerous. They bear the weight of the tabernacle on poles, step by step through sand and wilderness. They don't get to see the beauty they carry. Their work is faith in motion and obedience without spectacle. It's a vivid image of discipleship. So much of the Christian life is like this: carrying what we can't yet see, bearing the weight of grace wrapped in mystery, trusting that what we move for God's sake is precious beyond measure.

This story reminds us that holiness isn't confined to temples; it's also found in the sacred responsibilities entrusted to us. The work of love, justice, care, and truth-telling carries holy weight. To treat it carelessly is to risk spiritual collapse. Reverence is about devotion: a recognition that some things are so infused with God's presence that they demand our full attention, humility, and care.

For modern hearts, this passage critiques the culture of casualness that treats everything as ordinary. We've lost touch with the trembling awareness that once defined worship. We handle holy things (Scripture, prayer, liturgy, sacraments, creation, one another) without pause, without wonder. But the Kohathites remind us: the sacred must be borne with reverence, not convenience.

In Jesus, the tension between holiness and nearness is transfigured. The untouchable becomes touchable. The holy is no longer carried on poles, but walks among us, healing and blessing. Yet even now, that same reverence is required, as we embrace the awe of mystery and intimacy. Christ invites us to carry the presence of God within our own lives with the same careful joy the Kohathites carried the ark: never taking lightly what is eternally weighty.

Guiding Truth: The presence of God is both gift and fire, carried not with control but with reverent love and careful faithfulness.

Reflection: What sacred responsibilities has God entrusted to me that I may have treated too casually? How can I cultivate reverence in a world that's forgotten how to tremble at holy things?

Prayer: Holy One, teach me to carry your presence with care. Guard me from treating what's sacred as ordinary. Let my service, my love, and my faith bear the weight of reverence and joy, that your glory might rest gently upon all I do. Amen.

Day 7: The Grace of Carrying What's Yours

Reading: Numbers 4:21–49

God continues assigning the Levite clans their sacred tasks. The sons of Gershon and Merari are numbered: men aged thirty to fifty, strong enough to carry weight, steady enough to bear it faithfully. Their work? The unglamorous labor of transporting the tabernacle. Gershon's descendants handle the curtains, coverings, and cords: the woven skin of God's dwelling. Merari's family carries the frames, posts, bases, and crossbars: the bones that hold it all together.

It's holy work, though it doesn't sparkle. There's no spotlight here, no prestige, no priestly robes or public blessing. Just the sound of ropes tightening, poles creaking, dust rising, shoulders straining. The dwelling place of God moves through the wilderness because someone is willing to carry what's heavy and unseen.

The beauty of this passage lies in its theology of vocation. The Levites aren't interchangeable. Each clan is entrusted with a distinct portion of God's dwelling, and to abandon it would unravel the whole. What looks ordinary is indispensable. The sacred is sustained by the steady faithfulness of those who carry their part.

There's something profoundly subversive here. We live in a culture obsessed with visibility, where value is measured by applause, influence, and recognition. But God's economy is different. In God's kingdom, glory hides in the small, sacred acts that keep love alive: the ones no one else notices. The gospel always begins at ground level, in the calloused hands of those who shoulder the load with grace.

Every faithful act (whether carrying curtains or speaking truth, serving tables or preaching the Word) is a way of participating in divine movement. The Levites remind us that God's presence travels through the faithfulness of ordinary people who do their part without complaint or comparison.

There's another layer of grace here: no one carries everything. The burden is shared. The load of the tabernacle is distributed among the clans. Even the holy weight is communal. This is the rhythm of healthy community: each carrying what's ours, no more, no less, with reverence and cooperation. To take up another's load would dishonor their calling; to drop our own would dishonor God's.

Spiritually, this text calls us to discernment and humility. What has God asked me to carry? Maybe it's the unseen work of prayer, the simple labor of caregiving, the unheralded call of integrity in a dishonest world. It might feel small, but the journey of God's people depends on such hidden faithfulness.

The Levites moved the tabernacle one stage at a time, not rushing, not collapsing, guided by divine command. Similarly, we are called to bear the weight of love and justice, one day at a time, trusting that even our smallest obedience carries the presence of God into the world.

And when the journey ends, and the tent is raised again, every frame and fabric will testify: nothing carried in love was wasted.

Guiding Truth: God's presence moves through the faithfulness of ordinary people who carry their portion of holiness with humility and care.

Reflection: What small or hidden work of love has God entrusted to me in this season? How can I carry it with gratitude rather than resentment or comparison?

Prayer: God of shared burdens, teach me to carry what's mine with faithfulness and joy. Guard me from envy and exhaustion. Let every act of service, seen or unseen, be a way of bearing your presence into the world. Amen.

Day 8: When Holiness Touches the Wounds

Reading: Numbers 5:1–31

The wilderness is often a place of wandering, but it can also be a place of purification. In Numbers 5, God commands that the camp be kept clean, not out of moral fastidiousness, but because divine presence dwells among the people. "Command the Israelites to send away anyone who is ceremonially unclean," God says. This isn't about exclusion for exclusion's sake; it's about protection. The holy God has chosen to live among humans. For holiness to dwell in proximity to brokenness without consuming it, boundaries must be drawn. The purpose is to heal.

Then the chapter turns toward reconciliation. First, it speaks of restitution: making right what's been wronged. When someone has sinned against another, they must confess and repay, adding a fifth as a gesture of repentance. Holiness is relational. God's presence is sustained in a community where wrongs are owned and reparations made.

And then comes the passage that disturbs modern ears: the ordeal of the suspected adulteress. It's a complex text: a ritual in which a woman accused of unfaithfulness is brought before the priest, who mixes dust from the tabernacle floor with holy water and makes her drink it as a test of innocence or guilt. It feels strange, harsh, even unjust. It's a world unlike the modern one most of us inhabit, with beliefs and rituals that are completely foreign and strange.

Yet within its ancient context, this ritual was strangely protective. In surrounding cultures, suspicion of adultery often led to immediate violence. Here, however, God insists on a process: a public, priestly, and accountable act that removes the husband's right to take vengeance. The judgment belongs to God, not humans. The woman stands not before her accuser's rage but before the God who sees. It's not perfect justice as we long for it, but in a brutal world, it was mercy wrapped in ritual.

Still, the passage begs for completion. Its partial justice points forward to a greater revelation: the day when Jesus will stoop beside another woman accused of adultery, this time in the dust of a temple court. The men demand stoning; Jesus writes in the sand. The law that once condemned becomes fulfilled in mercy. "Let the one without sin cast the first stone." No stones fall. The woman rises, freed not by ritual but by grace.

Numbers 5 reminds us that holiness is the ongoing work of reconciliation: between bodies, communities, relationships, and God. The call to "send away" what is unclean was never about exclusion; it was about creating space where healing could occur. And healing comes not through fear but through truth, confession, and mercy.

We, too, are called to that same holiness, which confronts injustice without cruelty, names sin without dehumanizing sinners, and guards the community not through suspicion but through compassion. When holiness touches the wounds, healing begins.

Guiding Truth: Holiness is love that transforms brokenness into wholeness through truth, mercy, and grace.

Reflection: Where do I confuse holiness with avoidance rather than compassionate engagement? What would it look like for holiness to touch (not punish) the wounds in my life or community?

Prayer: Holy Presence, dwell among us even in our brokenness. Teach me a holiness that heals rather than harms, that confesses rather than conceals, that moves toward mercy instead of fear. Let your truth and compassion make my heart, and our community, whole. Amen.

Day 9: A Life Set Apart for Love

Reading: Numbers 6:1–21

The Nazirite vow is one of the most hauntingly beautiful moments in the wilderness story. It's voluntary, radical, and profoundly countercultural: a holy rebellion against the numbing rhythms of ordinary life. In a world driven by power, production, and self-preservation, the Nazirite chooses surrender. They dedicate their lives to serving Yahweh, pursuing consecrated ministry, and showing how dedication to God is characterized by holiness and relationship.

This vow can be taken by anyone: man or woman, rich or poor. It's a sacred democratization of holiness. For a time, or for a lifetime, the Nazirite sets themselves apart for God in visible and bodily ways. They refrain from wine and fermented drinks, which are symbols of comfort, indulgence, and forgetfulness. They let their hair grow, which is a mark of vulnerability, a public reminder that their strength comes not from grooming or control but from grace. And they avoid contact with death (even that of loved ones) to honor the life-giving presence of the Holy One who calls them.

These practices are about focus and dedication: an embodied protest against distraction. The Nazirite vow is a plunge into the reality of God's reign. In the wilderness of noise, this vow says: "I'll remember. I won't numb myself. I'll live awake to the presence of the Living God."

When the time of consecration ends, the Nazirite offers sacrifices and shaves their head, placing the hair (the physical sign of their vow) on the altar fire. The gesture is striking. What they once carried as a badge of devotion becomes an offering. It's a holy letting go, a reminder that even our consecration is a gift, not an achievement.

At its heart, this vow reveals that holiness isn't primarily about separation from what's impure, but about orientation toward what's good, noble, true, and God-glorifying. Holiness is sometimes considered a retreat from the world's temptations and mess. But the truth is that holiness is a different way of being in the world: letting God shape you into a living sign of an alternative kingdom.

In our time, the spirit of the Nazirite vow might look like simplicity, fasting from excess, cultivating silence in a culture of noise, or refusing the intoxication of power and acclaim. It might mean abstaining from whatever dulls our compassion or weakens our attention to God's voice: the digital wine, the constant consumption, the ceaseless proving of worth.

The prophetic edge of this passage cuts deep. It reminds us that devotion to God will always look strange to a world that worships comfort. The Nazirite's hair, wild and untamed, confronts our obsession with control and appearance. Their abstinence mocks the myth that satisfaction can be bought. Their solitude exposes how much we fear quiet.

Yet beneath the radical symbolism lies something tender. God invites anyone to draw near, to live differently for a season, to reorder love. Holiness is God's open invitation to embrace and reflect divine goodness and love.

And in Jesus, we glimpse the true Nazirite: not by vow but by essence. He lives fully consecrated, fully human, and wholly surrendered. His life is the ultimate offering, his love the fire that consecrates our hearts.

Guiding Truth: To be consecrated is to live awake: to resist numbness, embody love, and let every part of life become an offering to God.

Reflection: What might a Nazirite-like devotion look like in my season of life? What comforts, distractions, or indulgences might God be calling me to release to live more awake to love?

Prayer: God of consecration, teach me to live with focus and wonder. Free me from the false comforts that dull my soul. Let my life (its work, its relaxation, its love) be set apart for you, until every breath becomes worship and every act a reflection of your holiness. Amen.

Day 10: The Shine of God's Face

Reading: Numbers 6:22–27

After instructions about vows and purity, the book of Numbers pauses to speak blessing. It's as if, after the long weight of law and labor, God breathes. "Tell Aaron and his sons," the Lord says to Moses, "This is how you're to bless the people of Israel."

And then come words that have crossed millennia and languages, prayed at bedsides, spoken at baptisms, chanted in monasteries, and sung in sanctuaries across the world:

"The Lord bless you and keep you;
the Lord make his face shine upon you and be gracious to you;
the Lord lift up his face toward you and give you peace."

This is no casual benediction. It's a declaration of divine posture. Blessing, keeping, shining, graciousness, peace: each word describes how God turns toward the world. The blessing doesn't just ask for protection or prosperity; it reveals the very character of the One who blesses.

"The Lord bless you and keep you." This is the language of steadfast care. To be blessed is to be seen, not overlooked. To be kept is to be held, not abandoned. It's the assurance that even in wilderness, even in exile, we aren't lost to God's gaze.

"The Lord make his face shine upon you and be gracious to you." This is the radiance of relationship. In Hebrew thought, the shining of one's face is the warmth of presence, the glow of favor and intimacy. God's face doesn't burn in judgment here; it shines in grace. It's light that reveals, not blinds; love that illumines, not condemns.

"The Lord lift up his face toward you and give you peace." To lift one's face toward another is to acknowledge them, to restore dignity, to meet them eye to eye. This blessing culminates not in power, but in shalom: a word deeper than peace as absence of conflict. Shalom means wholeness, flourishing, harmony. It's the mending of the world, the restoration of creation to its true design.

This blessing is the heartbeat of divine intention. It's how God desires to relate to humanity: not through fear, but through favor; not through distance, but through delight. When the priest speaks these words, they aren't magic; they're ministry. The priest doesn't generate blessing; they channel it. God says, "So shall they put my name on the people, and I'll bless them." The divine name YHWH rests upon the community like light upon water.

For us, this blessing calls to mind the face of Christ. In him, the shining face of God takes flesh. In him, the favor, grace, and peace of God walk among us. When Jesus blesses children, forgives sinners, and breathes peace on frightened disciples, this ancient prayer finds its ultimate fulfillment.

Our vocation, then, is to live as carriers of that blessing and reflect the shine of divine mercy in our words, our work, and our presence. The world is starved for kindness, for eyes that lift rather than look away. To bear the name of God is to bless, not curse: to keep others with the same tenderness that has kept us.

Guiding Truth: The face of God shines not to expose our shame but to restore our dignity; God blesses us to become a blessing to others.

Reflection: Where do I need to let the light of God's gracious face heal my fear or shame? How can I reflect divine blessing toward others in small, intentional ways this week?

Prayer: God of shining mercy, lift your face toward me and make me whole. Let your light heal what's hidden, your peace still what's restless, and your grace move through me to bless others. May your name rest upon me, not as burden, but as radiant love. Amen.

Day 11: Gifts of Gratitude, Not Glory

Reading: Numbers 7:1–41

When the tabernacle is finally set up, when the ark rests within its veil and the lamps flicker in the sanctuary, the leaders of Israel come forward. Each tribe brings an offering, not for spectacle, but for service. Their gifts are tangible, practical, heavy with both metal and meaning: silver basins, golden dishes, oxen, carts. It's the longest chapter in Numbers, not because God delights in lists, but because the Spirit delights in remembrance.

The offerings may seem repetitive, but that repetition is the heartbeat of devotion. Each tribe brings the same gifts. No one tries to outshine the other. There's no competition for divine attention, no hierarchy of generosity. This isn't the empire's pageantry but the covenant's equality. In the kingdom of God, no tribe's gift is more holy than another's.

Moses receives their offerings and distributes them to the Levites, providing practical provisions for the sacred work of carrying the tabernacle. The carts and oxen go to Gershon and Merari, who bear the curtains and framework. The Kohathites, who carry the holy things, receive none, because their burden must rest on shoulders, not wheels. Even here, in the details of distribution, divine wisdom breathes: different callings, different provisions, one purpose.

What seems like a passage of logistics is actually a portrait of love. The people have come through bondage and wilderness. Now, in freedom, they give back. Their gifts aren't about transaction but

33

participation. They're saying, "This presence among us matters. We want to make room for this holy God who dwells in our midst." Gratitude takes shape in craftsmanship, weight, and substance. Worship becomes visible.

In our culture, generosity is often tied to visibility: to plaques, platforms, and recognition. But here, the leaders of Israel offer their treasures anonymously before the tent. No names are celebrated above others. Each offering is recorded with the same words, the same care. The text's repetition is its theology: in God's memory, every act of devotion counts equally.

There's beauty in this collective obedience. These are ordinary acts of faithfulness, displayed in the rituals and practices of a community. The tabernacle becomes not just God's dwelling, but theirs: a shared space built from shared giving. Holiness, it turns out, is a communal experience.

This story also points forward. When the Magi kneel before the Christ child, bringing gold, frankincense, and myrrh, they echo these wilderness leaders. True worship always takes material form. Love gives. And every gift, however simple, participates in the divine generosity that sustains creation.

Spiritually, Numbers 7 invites us to examine how we give, including our time, presence, and resources. Do we give for glory or gratitude? Are our offerings motivated by duty or delight? When we give from joy, we participate in the rhythm of God's heart: the One who gives life, breath, and grace without measure.

When each tribe had offered, the tabernacle gleamed with shared generosity. The place of meeting wasn't built by one, but by all. The same remains true today. The presence of God still dwells most vividly where a people give, not out of pressure, but out of love.

Guiding Truth: True worship isn't measured by magnitude but by faithfulness: each gift, offered in love, makes space for God to dwell among us.

Reflection: Where am I tempted to give for recognition rather than gratitude? How might I contribute to the presence of God in my community this week?

Prayer: Generous God, teach me the joy of giving without glory. Let my offerings (whether words, work, or resources) be acts of love, not performance. Knit my gifts into the life of your people, until your dwelling shines through our shared devotion. Amen.

Day 12: The Long Obedience of Love

Reading: Numbers 7:42–89

The list continues, each tribe bringing its gift, each offering identical to the last: a silver platter, a silver basin, a golden dish, animals for sacrifice. One by one, they come in a procession of faithfulness that spans twelve days. To modern eyes, it may seem repetitive and even tedious. But that's the point. Scripture slows here on purpose. The Holy Spirit lingers in the rhythm of repetition because faith itself is repetitive: an act of steady, ordinary devotion.

Every tribe brings the same gift, yet each one's offering is named. God receives each contribution as singular, not generic. Love is never anonymous. What we give to God in sincerity becomes sacred not because it's unique, but because it's wholehearted. Repetition, in this passage, is music. It's the song of equality in worship.

In a culture obsessed with originality and recognition, Numbers 7 offers a different kind of beauty: the holiness of consistency. The people don't compete for divine favor; they contribute to divine dwelling. Twelve tribes, twelve days, one God: this is a covenant in motion. The text reads like liturgy, reminding us that worship is less about novelty than about presence.

After the final offering, Moses enters the tabernacle to speak with God. And there, something miraculous happens. "When Moses entered the tent of meeting to speak with the Lord, he heard the voice speaking to him from between the two cherubim above the atonement cover." The voice of the Holy One echoes from the mercy seat, the center of grace and reconciliation. The sound that once thundered on Sinai now speaks from within the tabernacle.

The story comes full circle. The gifts of the tribes, the careful obedience, the communal participation, all culminate not in human glory but in divine nearness. The goal of all giving, all serving, all building is this: that God may dwell among us, and we may hear God's voice again.

There's profound humility here. God chooses to speak not through spectacle, but through the stillness that follows shared obedience. Revelation flows from community. Holiness descends through unity. The Spirit's presence doesn't arrive through one tribe's exceptionalism, but through the harmony of many hearts yielding to one purpose.

Spiritually, this passage teaches us that devotion isn't measured by grandeur but by endurance. The tabernacle was sustained not by bursts of passion but by patient repetition. Faith matures in the same way: not in moments of emotional height, but in the daily rhythm of returning, offering, listening.

When Moses hears the voice between the cherubim, it's as if the universe sighs in relief. God and humanity, once divided, now meet again through covenant and offering. Every silver basin, every golden dish has led to this moment of communion.

Our offerings today (acts of justice, compassion, generosity, or prayer) still echo that ancient rhythm. We give, not to earn God's favor, but to make space for divine presence in a weary world.

The repetition of holiness continues: each act of faith another verse in the long obedience of love.

Guiding Truth: Holiness grows not through grand gestures but through steady, shared obedience that makes space for God's presence to dwell.

Reflection: Where am I called to practice the slow, repetitive work of love even when it feels unseen? How can my daily acts of faithfulness become a place for God's voice to speak again?

Prayer: God of the long journey, teach me the holiness of repetition: the beauty of showing up, offering, serving, and waiting. Let my faith become steady and simple, woven into the rhythm of your presence. May my obedience make room for your voice to dwell. Amen.

Day 13: Light, Service, and the Rhythm of Renewal

Reading: Numbers 8:1–26

The wilderness tabernacle gleams with the flicker of fresh light. God speaks to Moses: "Speak to Aaron and say to him, when you set up the lamps, see that all seven lamps give light in front of the lampstand." The lampstand (hammered from pure gold, shaped like almond blossoms) stands as more than an ornament. It's symbol and sacrament: the light of divine presence shining upon the community.

Aaron's task is to keep the lamps burning continually, their light directed forward, illuminating the sacred space where God meets the people. In a world where darkness still threatens, the light is prophetic. The God who called light from chaos still commands light to shine in the wilderness. This illumination flows from obedience, from tending the flame.

After the lampstand comes the consecration of the Levites. They're washed, shaved, and set apart for service. Their cleansing is both physical and symbolic: a visible confession that those who serve the Holy must first allow the Holy to cleanse them. But notice the detail: the people of Israel lay hands on them before they're offered to God. The Levites don't serve alone or above the people; they serve on behalf of them, as living offerings. Their holiness is communal. Their ministry is shared.

This act of laying on hands is radical tenderness. The people who once built a golden calf now entrust others to carry their spiritual burdens. The community becomes co-responsible for holiness. Grace is never a private possession; it's a shared vocation.

God then describes how the Levites will assist Aaron and his sons, caring for the tabernacle, maintaining its rhythms, and guarding its sanctity. This division of labor might seem rigid, but it's actually relational. God organizes the sacred work so that no one bears it alone, and no one is without purpose. This is belonging.

Finally, God sets boundaries for the Levites' years of service. From age twenty-five to fifty, they labor actively in the tent. Afterward, they assist, but they no longer carry the heavy load. This rhythm honors both strength and rest. It recognizes that even sacred work has seasons, that faithful service must yield to renewal. The God who calls people to serve also calls them to stop. Holiness includes Sabbath.

This passage, with its lamps, washings, and age limits, feels distant from modern life. Yet its essence still speaks: light, service, and rest shape faithful living. We're called to tend the light of God's presence in our daily lives, to keep love burning when cynicism tempts us to extinguish it. We're called to serve not from ego but from consecration, remembering that holiness is shared, not self-made. And we're called to rest, trusting that God's work continues even when we step aside.

In Christ, this pattern comes alive. He's the light that never dims, the servant who washes feet, the Lord who rests and restores. To follow him is to live illuminated, consecrated, and renewed.

Guiding Truth: The life of faith is sustained by tending God's light, serving from holiness, and resting in grace.

Reflection: What lights in my life (faith, love, hope) need tending so they don't fade? How am I being invited into the balance of sacred work and holy rest?

Prayer: God of light and mercy, keep my heart burning with your presence. Cleanse me to serve with joy, and teach me the wisdom of rest. Let my daily rhythm reflect your grace: a life illuminated, consecrated, and at peace in your care. Amen.

Day 14: Remembering in Motion

Reading: Numbers 9:1–23

The wilderness people are called to remember. A year after leaving Egypt, the Lord commands them to keep the Passover. The tents of Israel are still pitched in the dust of Sinai, but memory reaches back to the night of deliverance: the lamb, the blood, the midnight cry, the freedom no one expected. Even in transition, they're to rehearse redemption.

God anchors them in story. The Passover is identity. They're who they are because of what God has done. The feast transforms memory into hope; it tells them that the same God who parted the sea still moves with them through the desert.

But not everyone can participate easily. Some are ceremonially unclean from contact with the dead. They approach Moses, longing not to be left out. "Why should we be kept from bringing the Lord's offering at its appointed time?" Their question is holy. It's not rebellion; it's hunger for belonging. And God answers with grace. Those who are unclean or on a distant journey may celebrate later. The law bends toward mercy. Holiness makes room.

This moment reveals something vital about the character of God: divine order never cancels divine compassion. The God of holiness is also the God of inclusion. The command to remember is extended to all who desire to draw near. It's a glimpse of the gospel before the gospel: a mercy that anticipates Christ's open table, where the broken and weary find welcome.

Then the focus shifts from feast to following. The cloud of God's presence settles over the tabernacle. By day it's a cloud; by night it burns with fire. Whenever the cloud lifts, the people move; whenever it settles, they stay. Whether the pause lasts two days or two years, they wait. God's presence sets their schedule.

This image of the cloud and fire is one of Scripture's most intimate portrayals of divine guidance. It's both mysterious and concrete; visible, yet unpredictable. The people can't plan their route; they can only watch and respond. It's a hard kind of faith: no map, no timeline, only trust. But it's also freeing. They're never lost because they're never alone.

In a restless world obsessed with control and progress, this passage is a mirror. We often want clarity more than communion, predictability more than presence. But the way of discipleship is the way of the cloud: moving when God moves, resting when God rests.

The cloud and the Passover together reveal the rhythm of spiritual life: remembering and moving. Memory keeps us grounded in grace; guidance keeps us dependent on presence. To live by both is to walk the wilderness with courage, knowing that the God who delivered us still leads us.

In Christ, the Passover becomes personal and the cloud becomes internal. The Lamb has been slain, and the Spirit now dwells within. The same Presence that led them by fire now burns in our hearts, teaching us to remember and to follow, day by day.

Guiding Truth: The life of faith is a rhythm of remembrance and responsiveness: anchored in God's past faithfulness and guided by God's present presence.

Reflection: Do I trust God's timing: to stay when God settles me and move when God stirs me? How might remembering my own "Passover" moments strengthen my trust in the present journey?

Prayer: Faithful God, anchor me in your story and lead me by your presence. Teach me to remember what you've done and to follow where you lead. Whether I move or rest, let my heart stay centered in your grace. Amen.

Day 15: When the Trumpets Sound

Reading: Numbers 10:1–36

The people in the wilderness are ready to move. The camp, once still beneath the cloud of God's presence, is called to journey forward. But before the first tent is struck or the first step taken, God commands the making of two silver trumpets. Their sound will guide the people: not the shouting of commanders, not the noise of chaos, but the clear, holy call of metal shaped for worship.

The trumpets are instruments of alignment. When both sound, the congregation gathers. When one sounds, the leaders come. When the tone changes, the camp moves. When the alarm blasts, the people prepare for battle. Every note is sacred. The sound organizes their life around divine intention.

This moment is liturgy. God is teaching people how to listen. The wilderness, with its hunger and uncertainty, can easily drown out holy direction. But the trumpets cut through the noise, reminding them that movement without listening isn't faith, it's folly.

The trumpets are silver, refined and resonant. They are made for clarity, for purity of sound. In Scripture, silver often symbolizes redemption. These instruments of movement are formed from the metal of deliverance. God is saying: "You won't move by your own command but by the voice of redemption."

Then the cloud lifts. The ark of the covenant (the visible sign of God's nearness) moves ahead, carried by the Levites. The tribes fall into their appointed order: Judah first, then the rest in sequence. The camp becomes a moving sanctuary, a body in motion whose heart is the presence of God.

It's a sacred choreography of trust. Every journey begins and ends with divine initiative. "At the command of the Lord, they set out, and at the command of the Lord, they camped." The people move because God goes before them.

Moses prays as the ark sets out: "Rise up, O Lord! Let your enemies be scattered!" It's not a cry of conquest but of confidence: faith that God will make a way where none exists. And when the cloud settles again, Moses prays: "Return, O Lord, to the countless thousands of Israel." Every movement begins and ends in prayer.

This passage speaks to our own disordered world. We live in an age of noise: everyone calling, selling, performing, and summoning. The challenge is discernment. We move constantly, but often without meaning. The trumpets of God still sound, but they are subtle now: heard in Scripture, silence, prayer, liturgy, conscience, study, solitude, and community. The Spirit still calls us to gather, to move, to act, but always from listening first.

Faith, at its core, is learning to recognize the sound of redemption amid the static of fear and ambition. To move with God is to hear the trumpet's call and rise when it sounds.

Every true journey of faith begins like this: with the courage to listen, the humility to follow, and the prayer that God's presence would shape both movement and rest.

Guiding Truth: God still calls the people of faith to move at the sound of redemption: to act, speak, and live in rhythm with divine presence.

Reflection: How do I discern the "trumpet call" of God amid the clamor of daily life? Am I willing to wait in silence until God's direction becomes clear?

Prayer: God of movement and mercy, teach me to listen for your call. When you rise, let me follow; when you rest, let me be still. Tune my heart to your rhythm, that my life might move only to the music of your redeeming love. Amen.

Day 16: The Hunger Beneath the Hunger

Reading: Numbers 11:1–9

The wilderness has a way of revealing what's inside us. When the Israelites left Egypt, they carried the treasures of deliverance and the memories of slavery. Freedom had been miraculous, but it was also disorienting. Now, surrounded by monotony and sand, they begin to complain. They reveal their hearts through their words.

Their lament starts small, as murmuring often does. The text says they "grumbled about their hardships in the hearing of the Lord." And when God's fire breaks out at the edges of the camp, they cry out to Moses, and the fire is quenched. But the murmuring doesn't end. It shifts, deepens, and grows teeth.

The people begin to crave what they left behind: the food of Egypt (and probably its lifestyles and certainties). They remember the fish, cucumbers, melons, leeks, onions, and garlic. They long not for slavery itself, but for its comforts. They're tired of manna, that mysterious bread from heaven; white, sweet, sustaining. "Our strength is dried up," they say. "There's nothing but this manna to look at."

The tragedy here is amnesia. They've forgotten what the manna means. Every morning, the dew-laced ground testifies to divine faithfulness. God feeds them daily, intimately, miraculously. Yet the gift that once astonished has become ordinary. What was once grace now feels like a burden. They've also forgotten what the comforts and delights of Egypt meant: slavery, bondage, and suffering.

This passage exposes something ancient and modern alike: the restless hunger that no food can fill. The people's cravings aren't really for fish or melons; they're for control, predictability, and nostalgia. Wilderness hunger is spiritual hunger wearing a physical disguise. It's the longing for a life that feels easier, safer, more familiar: even if it means returning to chains.

In our own wilderness seasons (times of waiting, uncertainty, simplicity), we face the same temptation. We tire of manna. We want variety, excitement, excess. We forget that dependence on God is liberation and true flourishing. The monotony of grace can feel unsatisfying to souls addicted to novelty.

Manna teaches us the daily rhythm of trust. It comes only for the day: no storage, no hoarding. It's an invitation to let go of the myth of self-sufficiency and receive provision as a relationship, not an entitlement. The question is never "Is there enough?" but "Do I trust the One who gives?"

God's response to the complaint will unfold in the verses that follow (with meat and consequences), but here, the Spirit lingers on the contrast between divine constancy and human craving. The manna is heaven's humility (simple, faithful, sustaining). The craving is earth's forgetfulness (loud, anxious, restless).

The wilderness remains a mirror. It reveals how quickly we turn blessings into boredom, how often we hunger for what enslaves us, how easily we despise the very provision that keeps us alive.

But grace persists. Each dawn, the manna still falls. God's faithfulness doesn't depend on our gratitude. The Bread of Heaven keeps descending (then and now) in mercy that refuses to abandon even the complaining heart.

Guiding Truth: True hunger is for divine presence; God's daily grace is enough, even when our desires shout otherwise.

Reflection: Where am I mistaking monotony for lack, when in fact God's steady grace surrounds me? What cravings distract me from recognizing daily manna as a sign of love, not limitation?

Prayer: Faithful God, forgive my restless hunger for more. Teach me to taste your mercy in the ordinary and to trust your provision one day at a time. Let my cravings be transformed into gratitude and my emptiness into communion with you. Amen.

Day 17: The Weight of the People and the Wind of the Spirit

Reading: Numbers 11:10–35

Moses has reached his breaking point. The wilderness has worn him down, not by storms or scarcity, but by the constant noise of complaint. The people wail for meat, their memories twisted by longing for Egypt's "abundance." The same mouths that once cried for deliverance now grumble against freedom. They're tired, unhappy, and restless people, looking for someone to blame. And Moses, weary and overwhelmed, turns his frustration toward God.

"Why have you brought this trouble on your servant?" he pleads. "Did I conceive all these people? Where can I get meat for all of them? If this is how you're going to treat me, put me to death right now." His words are raw, unvarnished, painfully human. Here's no sanitized piety, just exhaustion in prayer form.

And yet, God doesn't rebuke Moses for his honesty. The Holy listens. Out of Moses's despair, a new pattern of leadership emerges. God tells him to gather seventy elders: those already recognized for wisdom and character. "I'll take some of the Spirit that's on you and put it on them." Thanks to God's grace and wisdom, the burden of leadership is shared. Divine compassion meets human limitation not with scolding, but with structure.

When the Spirit falls, it spills over. Two men, Eldad and Medad, remain in the camp yet begin to prophesy. Joshua, anxious to preserve order, urges Moses to stop them. But Moses, in one of Scripture's most humble and prophetic replies, says, "Are you jealous for my sake? I wish that all the Lord's people were prophets and that the Lord would put his Spirit on them!"

This is the longing of the kingdom: the dream that the presence of God wouldn't be confined to one leader, one tent, one tribe, but poured out upon all. It's a vision that bursts its boundaries here in the desert and finds fulfillment generations later at Pentecost, when wind and fire descend again and the Spirit is shared without limit.

But the passage doesn't end in triumph. The people's craving still demands reckoning. God sends quail: an abundance beyond imagining. The meat falls like rain, piling up on the ground. The people gather greedily, finally sated. Yet as they eat, judgment comes. The place is named Kibroth Hattaavah: "graves of craving." What they demanded in excess becomes their undoing.

This story holds both comfort and warning. Comfort, because God meets despair with Spirit, and warning, because craving without gratitude leads to ruin. The Spirit sustains; indulgence consumes. The wilderness exposes the difference between hunger that deepens faith and hunger that devours it.

Moses learns what every weary servant must: no person can carry the work of God alone. The Spirit must rest upon many shoulders. The same breath that sustains him now sustains a community. God's answer to human limitation is always shared grace.

And the Spirit still blows through the camp (restless, generous, boundary-breaking), calling each of us to carry a portion of the holy burden, not in strength, but in shared dependence.

Guiding Truth: God meets exhaustion not with rebuke but with shared Spirit; what we can't carry alone, grace distributes among many hearts.

Reflection: What burdens am I trying to bear alone that God might be inviting me to share? How can I recognize and celebrate the Spirit's work in others rather than control it?

Prayer: Breath of God, fall fresh on weary hearts. Lift the weight I've carried too long alone, and teach me to trust your Spirit at work in others. Please save me from cravings that consume and fill me instead with the fire that sustains. Amen.

Day 18: When Jealousy Meets the Face of God

Reading: Numbers 12:1–16

The wilderness has a way of exposing the heart: not only of the people but of their leaders. Miriam and Aaron, pillars beside Moses, begin to speak against him. Their complaint starts as a critique of his Cushite wife, but the real issue runs deeper: "Has the Lord spoken only through Moses? Hasn't God also spoken through us?"

It's the oldest temptation among those who serve: to turn calling into competition. What begins as shared ministry can curdle into envy when another's authority or intimacy with God seems greater. Miriam and Aaron don't reject God; they resent proximity. Their words aren't rebellion but insecurity wrapped in self-justification.

But the text says something startling: "And the Lord heard it." God listens not only to prayer but to jealousy, not only to praise but to whispering. And then comes one of the most intimate lines in all Scripture: "Now Moses was very humble, more than anyone else on the face of the earth." Humility becomes the hinge of this story.

God calls the three siblings to the tent of meeting. The divine cloud descends: a symbol of both nearness and judgment. From its mist, God speaks, affirming that prophets receive visions and dreams, but with Moses, the relationship is face-to-face. "He is faithful in all my house." In other words: intimacy isn't entitlement; it's the fruit of trust.

Then the cloud lifts, and Miriam is stricken with leprosy, her skin turned white as snow. The symbolism cuts deep. She who judged another's skin now bears the mark of her own pride. It's not an arbitrary punishment; it's a mirror and mercy. Her condition externalizes the inner disease of jealousy.

Aaron, horrified, turns to Moses: "Please, my lord, don't hold this sin against us!" The irony is thick: the one they questioned now becomes their intercessor. And Moses, true to his character, prays the simplest and most profound prayer in Scripture: "O God, please heal her!" No vindication. No gloating. Just mercy.

God answers, but with consequence. Miriam will be healed, but she must remain outside the camp for seven days. The whole community waits. The journey halts until restoration is complete. Even divine forgiveness doesn't erase the communal ripple of sin. Holiness requires both grace and space for healing.

This story highlights an essential reality for spiritual communities today: jealousy among those who serve the same mission still wounds the body of Christ. We may cloak envy in critique, or mask competition as discernment, but God still hears the murmurs of the heart. What heals it is humility: the posture of Moses, who refuses to hold power as possession and intercedes even for those who question him.

Miriam's restoration at the story's end is grace embodied. The people don't move on without her. Holiness waits for reconciliation. Healing isn't private; it's communal. The same cloud that judged now shelters again.

Guiding Truth: God's presence exposes jealousy but restores through humility; the community moves forward only when mercy triumphs over pride.

Reflection: Where might envy or comparison be distorting my service to God or others? What would it look like to pray for those who've criticized or misunderstood me?

Prayer: God of mercy, quiet my envy and heal my pride. When I'm tempted to compare, please remind me of your unique call on every life. Teach me humility that intercedes rather than resents, and make our communities whole through grace and patience. Amen.

Day 19: The Giants and the Grapes

Reading: Numbers 13:1–33

The long journey through the wilderness reaches a turning point. God tells Moses to send twelve spies (one from each tribe) to explore the land of promise. After months of wandering, this moment is thick with anticipation. Freedom is no longer a dream; it's within sight. The spies are told to see the land's goodness (its fruit, people, and cities) and to bring back a taste of what God has promised.

They go north, through the desert and valleys, all the way to Hebron. There they find abundance beyond imagination: clusters of grapes so large they must be carried on a pole between two men. The land is lush and alive, a tangible fulfillment of God's word. But alongside the abundance, they also see something else: giants. The cities are fortified, the inhabitants strong. What was supposed to be a vision of promise becomes a mirror of fear.

When the spies return, they hold both realities in their hands: fruit and fear, hope and hesitation. "It's indeed a land flowing with milk and honey," they report, "but the people are powerful, and the cities are fortified and very large." Ten voices dominate the conversation, magnifying threat over promise. "We seemed like grasshoppers in our own eyes," they say, "and we looked the same to them."

Fear reshapes perception. It doesn't just make enemies larger; it makes the self smaller. The spies forget who they are and whose they are. The wilderness has taught them dependence, but not yet trust. Their imagination collapses under the weight of anxiety.

Only two (Caleb and Joshua) see differently. Caleb silences the crowd: "Let's go up at once and take possession, for we are well able to overcome it." His courage is faith in the One who called them. Where others see giants, he remembers grace. Where others measure power, he recalls presence.

This story lays bare a truth that still cuts to the heart: the most significant barrier to promise isn't opposition but fear. God doesn't ask Israel to be fearless, only faithful: to move forward trusting that the divine presence outweighs human threats. But fear has a way of masquerading as realism, of sounding prudent, even wise. Ten spies spoke what seemed sensible, and a generation lost their inheritance.

The giants still stand in our world today: injustice, greed, violence, despair. And the church, like Israel, must decide what story to believe. The choice is always between the fruit and the fear, between trusting the God of abundance or succumbing to the narrative of scarcity.

Faith, as Caleb shows us, is a form of memory. Faith is remembering that the God who parted seas can surely bring us through fortified cities.

And here the story bends toward Jesus, who faced the true giants (sin and death) and entered their strongholds unarmed, save for love. His resurrection is the ultimate cluster of grapes: the first fruit of the world remade, the promise that the land ahead is good.

Guiding Truth: Fear magnifies the giants; faith remembers the fruit: God's promise is greater than whatever looms before us.

Reflection: What "giants" have I allowed to shrink my imagination of what God can do? How might I practice Caleb's courage: to see promise where others see impossibility?

Prayer: God of courage and abundance, free me from the tyranny of fear. Help me remember your past faithfulness and trust your future grace. When I see giants, lift my eyes to the fruit of your promise and teach me to walk forward in faith. Amen.

Day 20: When Fear Drowns Faith

Reading: Numbers 14:1–25

Night has fallen, but the camp of Israel doesn't sleep. The people who once wept for deliverance now weep for Egypt. The wailing spreads from tent to tent like wildfire. The reports of the spies have brought despair. In their grief and fear, they turn against Moses and Aaron. The wilderness echoes with rebellion: "If only we had died in Egypt! Or in this wilderness!" They talk of choosing a new leader and going back.

This isn't just a complaint; it's apostasy. They are ready to trade promise for predictability, freedom for familiarity. It's a chilling moment in the story of faith: when fear eclipses memory, and the gift of freedom feels like a curse.

Moses and Aaron fall facedown before the assembly. Caleb and Joshua tear their clothes (a sign of anguish and reverence) and plead with the people: "The land is exceedingly good! If the Lord is pleased with us, he'll bring us into it. Don't rebel or fear." Their faith is fierce, but the crowd won't hear it. Fear always drowns out reason. Stones are lifted, ready to silence the faithful few.

Then the glory of the Lord appears. The cloud that had led them now descends in judgment. God's voice trembles with grief: "How long will these people treat me with contempt? How long before they believe me, after all the signs I have done among them?" The ache behind those words is unmistakable. This is divine heartbreak, not wrath for wrath's sake.

God speaks of wiping them out and starting anew with Moses: a second creation, a do-over. But Moses stands in the breach. He becomes what Christ will one day embody: an intercessor who refuses to abandon the guilty. "If you destroy them," Moses pleads, "the nations will say you couldn't finish what you began." Then, with daring intimacy, he calls on the very heart of God: "The Lord is slow to anger, abounding in love, forgiving sin and rebellion . . . "

Moses reminds God of God's own character: a remarkable act of faith. And God relents. God won't destroy the people, but their generation won't enter the land. They'll wander until the fearful hearts have faded and new trust has been born. Their children, whom they thought doomed, will inherit the promise. Even in judgment, mercy has the final word.

This story is no ancient tragedy; it's a mirror. Every generation faces this crisis of faith: will we move forward into God's promise, or retreat into the slavery of fear? Fear masquerades as wisdom, but it's the death of trust.

And yet, the same God who judged still led them by cloud and fire. The same mercy that spared them still spares us. In Christ, the greater Moses, God's heart is forever turned toward intercession, not destruction.

Faith may falter, but grace remains steadfast. The call still stands: move forward.

Guiding Truth: Fear may delay the promise, but faith (even trembling faith) still calls us forward into mercy.

Reflection: Where am I tempted to turn back to what feels safe rather than trust God's forward call? How might I, like Moses, stand in the breach for others when they lose heart?

Prayer: Merciful God, forgive my backward gaze when fear drowns faith. Teach me to remember your goodness and walk toward your promise, even when the way is unclear. Let your mercy lead, your presence sustain, and your Spirit keep me moving forward in trust. Amen.

Day 21: The Tragedy of Presumptuous Faith

Reading: Numbers 14:26–45

The wilderness has turned heavy with consequence. The cries of rebellion have faded, replaced now by silence, the kind that follows grief and regret. God speaks again to Moses and Aaron, and the verdict is devastating: "How long will this wicked community grumble against me?" Every complaint, every word of distrust, has been heard. Now those very words become their judgment: "As surely as I live, declares the Lord, I'll do to you the very things I heard you say."

They had wished for death in the wilderness and, so, in the wilderness, they will die. Not as a cruel punishment, but as a sobering reality: a generation unable to trust won't inherit what trust alone can receive. The promise will still stand, but it will wait for children who have learned faith through wandering.

This passage cuts deep because it names a truth we prefer to ignore: not all regret leads to repentance. Israel mourns, but their sorrow is thin. It's grief for loss, not for sin. When Moses relays God's words, they respond with a sudden burst of zeal: "We'll go up to the place the Lord promised!" But the divine presence has already departed. Moses warns them: "Don't go up, for the Lord isn't with you. You'll be defeated."

Still, they go. Presumption takes the place of rebellion, as if religious enthusiasm could undo disobedience. They march toward the hill country without the ark, without Moses, without the presence that alone gives power. The result is heartbreak. The Amalekites and Canaanites sweep down and strike them. The same people who refused to enter the land in fear now try to seize it in pride, and both postures fail.

It's a haunting reversal. Fear kept them from entering when God said, "Go." Presumption drove them forward when God said, "Wait." Faith is neither of these. It's the alignment of will to divine presence, the readiness to move or stay according to love's leading.

This story isn't just about ancient Israel. It names something painfully human: the pendulum swing between despair and presumption. One day, we're paralyzed by fear; the next, we rush ahead without listening. Both are rooted in self-reliance, not trust. The wilderness is where God teaches a slower rhythm of dependence, discernment, and obedience shaped by presence, not impulse.

And yet, even here, grace hums beneath the text. The same God who judges will still feed them with manna, still guide them by cloud and fire, still bring their children home. The failure is real, but it's not final. The wilderness becomes their classroom, not their grave alone.

In Christ, this story finds its answer. The One who trusted perfectly in the Creator's will entered our wilderness of fear and presumption. Where we falter, grace remains steadfast.

Faith's most genuine courage isn't in seizing the promise but in staying near the Presence.

Guiding Truth: Presumption and fear are two faces of the same unbelief; faith learns to move only with the Presence of God.

Reflection: Where in my life have I confused zeal with obedience, rushing ahead of God's leading? How might I practice the patient trust that listens before acting?

Prayer: Faithful God, teach me to walk in step with your presence. Guard me from fear that freezes and pride that rushes ahead. In moments of regret, turn me toward repentance, not presumption. Let your Spirit shape my obedience into humble, courageous trust. Amen.

Day 22: Grace in the Wake of Failure

Reading: Numbers 15:1–21

The dust of rebellion has barely settled. The echoes of weeping still linger in the camp. Israel has watched an entire generation condemned to wander. The dream of Canaan seems lost; their future is shrouded in a wilderness haze. And then, out of the silence, God speaks again: but not with judgment, with promise.

"Speak to the Israelites and say to them: When you enter the land I am giving you to settle in."

It's almost impossible to overstate the grace of that opening line. When you enter, not if. The generation of unbelief may perish, but God's promise doesn't. The covenant still stands. Mercy is still writing the story. Out of the ashes of failure comes a new word of faithfulness: the future isn't canceled.

This passage, though it may read like a set of ritual instructions about offerings, is actually a declaration of hope. God gives Israel detailed directions for worship once they reach the land, specifying that grain, oil, and wine are to be brought alongside burnt offerings and fellowship sacrifices. Each act of worship will embody gratitude: a tangible remembrance that every harvest, every loaf, every drop of wine is a gift.

For a people who have lost their way, these words are more than liturgical detail; they're a reorientation. The rituals remind Israel that worship isn't just about atonement; it's about belonging. God is saying: "You'll have a home again. You'll bake bread from your own grain.

You'll drink from your own vineyards. And when you do, you will remember me."

The wilderness had been a place of scarcity and complaint. But God is already teaching them how to live in abundance without forgetting the Source. Every offering of flour and oil becomes a counter-liturgy against forgetfulness. It's as if God is planting seeds of faith long before they touch the soil of promise.

And here, something profound unfolds: worship becomes a form of resistance. Gratitude becomes a discipline of hope. In a world that trains us to measure worth by control, productivity, and possession, these ancient offerings remind us that everything we hold is a gift. Faithfulness isn't only about surviving the wilderness; it's about learning how to receive the promise rightly, without letting abundance turn into arrogance.

This passage also carries an inclusivity. God commands that these practices apply not only to native-born Israelites but also to the foreigners among them who share in the worship of God. From the beginning, the covenant was never meant to be tribal. Grace continually widens the circle.

Even after failure, God doesn't erase the people's story; God re-centers it. Sin has consequences, yes, but grace has continuity. The God of the wilderness still prepares a feast.

And here the story bends toward Jesus: the one who turns water into wine and multiplies bread in the desert. Every offering in Numbers points to him: the grain of his body, the wine of his blood, the oil of his anointing poured out for the renewal of the world.

Grace doesn't forget. It restores.

Guiding Truth: Even after failure, God continues to speak promises; grace writes the next chapter before we deserve it.

Reflection: Where have I mistaken consequence for abandonment, forgetting that God still speaks when, not if? How can gratitude become my act of resistance in a culture obsessed with ownership and control?

Prayer: God of promise, speak hope into my wilderness. Teach me to live as one who receives, not hoards. In every harvest, please remind me of your grace. In every loss, renew my trust. Let my worship be gratitude made visible, and my life a testimony of mercy that never ends. Amen.

Day 23: Threads of Remembrance

Reading: Numbers 15:22–41

The wilderness remains a place of contradiction: failure and faith, judgment and mercy, despair and new beginnings. After the rebellion, God continues to shape Israel through the laws of restoration. Numbers 15:22–41 might appear at first as dry legal detail, but under its surface beats the steady pulse of grace.

This passage deals with sin, specifically, sin done "unintentionally." It acknowledges the frailty of human hearts: that we forget, we drift, we act before we think. God doesn't treat these lapses as rebellion, but as weakness in need of healing. There's provision for atonement, for the individual and for the whole community. It's a vision of mercy large enough to hold both personal failure and collective complicity.

But then comes a striking contrast: a man who acts "defiantly," gathering wood on the Sabbath in open disregard of divine instruction. His punishment (death) is shocking to modern ears, but the text's weight lies not in cruelty, but in consequence. It warns that deliberate rejection of God's rhythm (Sabbath, rest, dependence) leads to self-destruction. The wilderness teaches that freedom without reverence collapses into chaos.

Yet even in this moment of severity, grace refuses to fade. God instructs Moses to tell the people to make tassels on the corners of their garments, woven with a thread of blue. Every time they look at the tassels, they are to remember all of God's commands and keep them.

It's a profoundly tender gesture. God, who has seen their forgetfulness, gives them a physical reminder, a thread to anchor them in covenant memory, not as a superstition, but as a sacrament: a visible sign of invisible grace. The blue cord, echoing the color of the sky, ties their daily lives to heaven's faithfulness.

Memory becomes the means of transformation. The tassels remind Israel who they are and whose they are. Forgetfulness, in Scripture, is never just a mental lapse: it's spiritual drift, the slow erosion of a relationship. God's antidote is simple, embodied, and communal: remember.

Our age knows something of this danger. We, too, live amid distractions that fragment attention and erode memory of what truly matters. The blue thread still calls us: not as ancient law, but as spiritual posture. To remember God's covenant is to resist the amnesia that comes with a culture addicted to novelty. To wear the memory of divine mercy close to our bodies is to anchor ourselves in faithfulness when everything around us tempts us to forget.

The chapter closes with a reaffirmation of identity: "I'm the Lord your God, who brought you out of Egypt to be your God." Grace is rooted in history, in deliverance, in a love that liberates before it commands.

In Christ, we see the blue thread made flesh: the living reminder of God's faithfulness woven into our world. His Spirit now inscribes the law on our hearts. The call remains the same: remember, and live.

Guiding Truth: God weaves reminders of grace into our ordinary days so that memory may become the seedbed of faithfulness.

Reflection: What threads of remembrance help me stay grounded in God's presence amid distraction and forgetfulness? How can I embody remembrance in my relationships, choices, and acts of justice and mercy?

Prayer: God of mercy and memory, tie my restless heart to your faithfulness. In moments of distraction, draw me back to your love. Let every act, every breath, every rhythm of my day become a blue thread that remembers your grace. Amen.

Day 24: The Earth That Swallowed Pride

Reading: Numbers 16:1–35

The wilderness isn't merely a landscape; it's a crucible for hearts. By now, Israel has seen fire, manna, and mercy. They've heard the voice of God and witnessed both promise and discipline. Yet still, pride brews beneath the surface.

Korah, a Levite from the same tribe as Moses, rises up with Dathan, Abiram, and two hundred and fifty leaders of Israel. Their protest begins with a truth twisted by envy: "All the community is holy, every one of them, and the Lord is with them. Why then do you set yourselves above the assembly?"

It sounds democratic, even righteous. But beneath their words lies resentment, not justice. They mistake equality for autonomy. They confuse access to God with authority over God's calling. Their rebellion is about control.

Moses, weary yet wise, falls facedown, appealing to God's presence. "In the morning," he says, "the Lord will show who belongs to him." His posture is striking: humility in the face of arrogance. Moses knows leadership in God's kingdom is received and surrendered daily.

Korah and his followers persist. They want proof, spectacle, validation. The wilderness has made them restless. They view leadership as a privilege, not a burden. Moses pleads again: "Isn't it enough that the God of Israel has separated you to serve in the tabernacle? Must you also seek the priesthood?" His voice trembles with grief. Ambition has closed their eyes to grace.

Then the earth groans. The ground beneath their feet opens like a wound and swallows the rebels whole. Fire consumes those offering unauthorized incense. It's a terrifying scene, but its center isn't cruelty; it's holiness. The earth itself bears witness that creation can't sustain the weight of pride. When humans defy divine order to exalt themselves, the ground gives way beneath them.

This story unsettles because it mirrors our age. We, too, live in a world where ambition disguises itself as virtue, where spiritual authority becomes a spectacle, and where power is mistaken for calling. The rebellion of Korah warns that spiritual leadership divorced from humility leads only to collapse. The earth may not open literally, but communities, institutions, and hearts crumble all the same.

And yet, even here, grace is present. The next chapter will tell of Aaron's staff budding with new life, proof that God's chosen leadership brings fruit, not fire. Divine judgment is never God's last word; renewal always follows ruin.

This passage calls us to reimagine leadership: not as hierarchy or entitlement, but as service grounded in surrender. The God who shook the earth in judgment now stoops in Christ to wash feet. Holiness still demands reverence, but it's revealed through humility, not pride.

Guiding Truth: Pride seeks power in God's name; humility carries power in God's presence.

Reflection: Where might I be resisting the way God chooses to lead through others or through weakness? How can I practice the kind of leadership that bends low, listening before speaking, serving before ruling?

Prayer: Holy One, keep me from the rebellion of pride that forgets your grace. Root me in humility, in the humble confidence that your presence is enough. Where I seek control, teach surrender; where I crave status, form me into a servant. Amen.

Day 25: Standing Between the Living and the Dead

Reading: Numbers 16:36–50

The ground has closed. The smoke has cleared. But the wounds of rebellion still hang thick in the air. Israel stands trembling, haunted by what has just happened: the earth swallowing Korah's company, the fire consuming the two-hundred-and-fifty who offered unauthorized incense. You'd think the people would fall silent in awe and repentance. Instead, by the next day, they accuse Moses and Aaron: "You've killed the Lord's people."

Grief, fear, and confusion twist into accusation. It's a tragedy as old as humanity: when hearts can't face their own complicity, they project blame onto others. The camp murmurs, and once again, the presence of God descends. A plague breaks out among the people. Death moves like wildfire.

But here the story shifts: from rebellion to redemption, from judgment to intercession. God tells Moses to step aside, but Moses doesn't retreat. He turns to Aaron and says, "Take your censer, put incense in it, and run into the midst of the assembly to make atonement for them."

And Aaron runs. The old priest, who once shaped a golden calf, now carries fire from the altar (the fire of mercy) into the heart of the dying camp. As he stands between the living and the dead, the plague stops. The image is unforgettable: one frail human standing in the breach, holding up the smoke of prayer between wrath and ruin.

This moment reveals the very heart of priesthood: not ceremony, but costly compassion. Aaron doesn't wait for the people to repent. He doesn't argue theology. He moves toward suffering with holy urgency. The censer in his hands becomes a bridge of grace.

This scene marks a pivotal moment in Israel's wilderness journey. It reminds us that holiness isn't only separation from sin but also movement toward mercy. The same fire that once consumed now purifies. The priest who once failed now becomes the vessel of intercession.

In every generation, God seeks such intercessors: those willing to step between destruction and deliverance, blame and healing, judgment and grace. We see them in prophets who speak truth with tears, in leaders who pray for those who curse them, in disciples who bear witness in dark places. And ultimately, we see it in Jesus: the Great High Priest who runs into the plague of sin itself, bearing not incense but his own life. On the cross, he stands between the living and the dead, and the plague stops.

This passage, raw and sobering, calls us back to the ministry of intercession. Our world still teeters between life and death, conflict and peace, despair and hope. The invitation is clear: take up the censer, draw near to the suffering, and let the fragrance of grace fill the space where judgment once burned.

Guiding Truth: True holiness doesn't flee from the broken; it runs toward them with the fire of mercy.

Reflection: Where might God be calling me to stand "between the living and the dead" in prayer, presence, or compassion? How can I let mercy, not fear, guide my response to the pain and rebellion of others?

Prayer: God of compassion, teach me to carry your mercy into the places of pain and despair. Make my life an offering of intercession, a living bridge of love. Where judgment looms, let grace rise like incense and bring healing to the broken. Amen.

Day 26: The Staff That Blossomed

Reading: Numbers 17:1–13

The wilderness still hums with unease. The ground has swallowed rebels, and fire has devoured pretenders. Even after mercy halted the plague, fear lingers. The people cry out to Moses, "We'll die! We're lost! Everyone who approaches the tabernacle will perish!"

They've seen holiness, but they don't yet understand it. They know God's power but not God's heart. So once again, God teaches: not through punishment this time, but through a living sign.

God instructs Moses to gather twelve staffs, one for each tribe, and write the name of each tribal leader upon it. Aaron's name is written on the staff of Levi. These dead sticks (symbols of human authority) are placed before the ark in the Tent of Meeting. God promises that the one chosen will sprout.

It's a simple act. No fire, no thunder, no voice from the cloud. Just silence and waiting.

When Moses returns the next day, something has happened. Aaron's staff (once dry wood like all the others) hasn't only sprouted but also blossomed and borne ripe almonds. Life has broken through death. The symbol of authority has become a sign of fruitfulness.

This is how God reveals divine calling: not through coercion or fear, but through generative life. In a world where power so often crushes and controls, God's authority gives life, beauty, and nourishment. The staff doesn't burn; it blooms.

Moses brings the rods before the people, and they see the difference for themselves. Then God commands that Aaron's staff be placed permanently before the ark: a witness against grumbling, a reminder that authentic leadership is measured not by position, but by fruit.

The message cuts deep: real spiritual authority is never self-proclaimed. Charisma, credentials, or conquest do not secure it. It's confirmed by the presence of life where death once reigned. The one God chooses will always bear fruit that blesses others, not wounds them.

This sign also heals something broken. After so much fear, the people need to see that holiness isn't only fire, it's fertility. God's presence both consumes and cultivates. The same God who judged rebellion now plants a promise of renewal.

For us, Aaron's staff becomes a living parable. It points beyond itself to Jesus: the true High Priest whose authority is rooted in love, surrender, crucifixion, divinity, and resurrection. The cross, like the staff, looked lifeless, dry, stripped of glory. Yet from that dead wood, life blossomed for the world.

When the church forgets this, it drifts toward the spirit of Korah: grasping for power, confusing noise with fruit, and mistaking control for calling. However, the Spirit continually draws us back to the staff that blooms. The mark of divine presence is always life that heals, nourishes, and multiplies.

Guiding Truth: True spiritual authority doesn't burn, it blossoms; God's chosen always bring life where death once ruled.

Reflection: Where have I confused power with fruitfulness in my life or community? What might it look like to let resurrection life, not human ambition, define my calling and leadership?

Prayer: God of life, make my heart like Aaron's staff: rooted in your presence, blossoming in your grace. Teach me to lead through gentleness, to bear fruit in humility, and to trust that proper authority is always born of love. Amen.

Day 27: The Weight and Gift of Sacred Work

Reading: Numbers 18:1–32

After the earth has opened and the staff has blossomed, God turns to Moses and Aaron with a steadier word. The drama of rebellion gives way to instruction, to the long obedience that sustains a people. The Lord speaks to Aaron about vocation: the call to bear responsibility for the sanctuary and priesthood. It's a sacred charge, but also a sober one: "You and your sons will bear the guilt connected with the sanctuary and the priesthood."

This is a calling that carries both weight and wonder. The priest stands in a holy tension: close to glory, yet surrounded by human fragility. Holiness, as Israel is learning, is about being in close proximity to God. To draw near to God is to carry the burdens of others, to live on behalf of the people with reverence and humility.

God assigns the Levites to assist the priests, to guard the tabernacle, and serve its rhythms of worship. They are custodians of sacred space: protectors, singers, carriers, and servants. Their ministry is often unseen: lifting curtains, tending fires, bearing the ark through desert miles. Yet in God's economy, these hidden acts sustain the life of the community.

Then comes a surprising twist. God tells Aaron and the Levites that they'll receive no inheritance of land like the other tribes. Instead, God says: "I'm your portion and your inheritance." What a staggering statement. The others will inherit territory, crops, and boundaries; the priests will inherit the very presence of God. Their livelihood will come from the offerings of the people: the tithes, grain, and sacrifices brought in worship.

In a world driven by possession and control, this word feels radical. To have God as one's portion means to live by grace, humility, and integrity. It's a call to trust, to find sufficiency not in wealth or acclaim, but in divine communion. What seems like loss becomes abundance.

This chapter redefines vocation as stewardship. Each person, each tribe, each calling has its place in the divine symphony. The priestly work, the Levite's labor, the farmer's tithe: all interwoven into a community sustained by mutual trust and holy dependence.

We need this reminder. The church today still wrestles with the temptations of entitlement, hierarchy, and self-importance. But the priesthood of all believers calls each of us into the same posture God demanded of Aaron: service rooted in reverence, ministry born of mercy, leadership marked by love.

This passage points forward to Jesus, the true High Priest, who bore the full weight of humanity's guilt and offered himself as the ultimate, perfect sacrifice. His inheritance wasn't land but love; not silver or gold, but a kingdom without borders.

To serve God, then, isn't to climb higher; it's to bend lower. To minister is to serve, surrender, sacrifice, and belong.

Guiding Truth: The holiest calling is service: living as one whose only inheritance is the presence of God.

Reflection: How might I rediscover my vocation, not as ambition or duty, but as gift and grace? What does it mean for me to live as one who truly believes that God alone is my portion?

Prayer: God of calling and compassion, teach me the beauty of holy responsibility. Guard me from pride and self-importance. Let your presence be my inheritance and your service my joy. In every task, hidden or seen, let me bear the weight of love with faithfulness. Amen.

Day 28: Ashes of Cleansing

Reading: Numbers 19:1–22

The wilderness is a place of dust: grit beneath the feet, ashes in the air, mortality everywhere. It's here, amid fragility and decay, that God gives one of the most enigmatic instructions in all of Scripture: the ritual of the red heifer.

A flawless red cow, never yoked or burdened, is brought outside the camp. It's sacrificed: not on the altar, not in the sanctuary, but in the open, beyond the sacred boundaries. Its blood is sprinkled toward the tabernacle, its body burned completely with cedar, hyssop, and scarlet wool. The ashes are then gathered and mixed with running water to create a cleansing solution. Paradoxically, the same ashes that purify others render those who handle them "unclean."

It's a ritual of paradox and poetry, a choreography of dust and grace. What defiles also heals. What burns becomes medicine. Purity is born from ashes.

The red heifer stands as a sign that holiness isn't about separation from the world's mess, but about God's willingness to meet us in it. The camp of Israel was full of death: bodies buried in the desert, mortality woven into daily life. This ritual was about reestablishing a connection to communion. When someone touched death, they weren't cast out forever. They could be restored, washed, and welcomed.

This is grace in motion, a God who refuses to let death have the final word. Even in the wilderness, where every loss was a reminder of fragility, God created a rhythm of cleansing that restored dignity to the grieving and the unclean.

The paradox continues: those who prepared the ashes became unclean themselves. In other words, the ones who helped others find purification bore the cost of defilement. It's a foreshadowing of the gospel; of the One who would step outside the camp, bear our impurity, and turn death itself into the means of redemption.

This strange ritual, full of ancient symbols and desert dust, offers the same truth that the cross later shouts: holiness is costly love. It's not about withdrawal from the broken, but about entering their suffering to bring healing. The red heifer's ashes are a sign that God's grace reaches where life has collapsed.

We live in a culture that hides from death, masks pain, and denies weakness. But this text invites us to face mortality not with fear, but with faith in the God who transforms ashes into cleansing water. When we face our own frailty, we discover not contamination but compassion.

And here, again, the story bends toward Christ. Outside the city walls, beyond the sacred boundaries, Jesus was crucified: the spotless one who bore impurity to make us whole. The ashes of the heifer find their fulfillment in his cross: the place where defilement becomes the doorway to restoration.

Guiding Truth: Holiness is God's power to bring life through death, as shown in the crucifixion and resurrection of Jesus Christ.

Reflection: Where do I need to let God meet me "outside the camp," in the place of my fear or failure? How can I become an agent of cleansing grace, entering others' pain without fear of defilement?

Prayer: God of ashes and mercy, meet me in my dust. Turn what is burned and broken into the soil of new life. Teach me the holiness that bears another's burden and transforms death into resurrection hope. Amen.

Day 29: Water from the Rock, Tears in the Dust

Reading: Numbers 20:1–13

The wilderness has become a familiar, painful setting. Death and dust. Wandering and waiting. And now, sorrow strikes again: "Miriam died there and was buried." With her passing, a generation begins to fade. The prophetess who sang by the sea now rests in desert sand.

Almost immediately, another crisis comes. The people have no water. The old chorus of complaint rises again: "Why did you bring us here to die? Why did we ever leave Egypt?" It's a painful refrain, so familiar that it cuts Moses to the bone. He's grieving, weary, and surrounded by unending demand.

Moses and Aaron fall facedown before the Tent of Meeting. The glory of the Lord appears, and the divine voice speaks: "Take the staff, assemble the community, and speak to the rock before their eyes, and it will pour out its water."

But something in Moses snaps. Years of burden, frustration, and unrelenting leadership fatigue break open. Instead of speaking to the rock, he strikes it twice with his staff. The water gushes forth, the people drink, and the livestock are saved. Outwardly, it looks like success. But inwardly, something sacred has been breached.

Then comes the divine word: "Because you didn't trust me enough to honor me as holy before the people, you won't bring this community into the land I give them."

It's one of the most haunting moments in Scripture. After decades of faithfulness, Moses falters: not in public scandal, but in subtle defiance. His sin isn't that he struck the rock instead of speaking, but that he turned obedience into performance. In anger, he makes himself the actor of the miracle, saying, "Listen, you rebels, must we bring you water from this rock?" The "we" betrays the heart. In pain and exhaustion, Moses takes ownership of what was always a gift of grace.

This passage reminds us that holiness is about surrender and trusting in God. When we act out of fear, resentment, or ego, even when doing good, we misrepresent the character of God. Moses's anger turned a moment of mercy into one of pride. Yet even in disobedience, the rock still pours forth water. Grace flows through cracked vessels. The people's thirst is quenched, even as their leader breaks.

This story invites deep compassion. Moses's failure is human. He's tired, grieving, carrying too much for too long. And God's response, though severe, is mercy. The promise continues; the people still drink. But holiness can't be reduced to outcomes; it's about the posture of the heart.

Centuries later, Paul will write that the Rock in the wilderness was Christ. He was struck once for all, so that living water might flow forever. Moses's staff reminds us of the cost of striving; the Rock reminds us of the sufficiency of grace.

At Meribah, holiness and mercy meet in tension. The water still flows. So does grace.

Guiding Truth: God's grace still flows through human failure, but holiness calls us to trust rather than strive.

Reflection: Where might exhaustion or anger be distorting the way I represent God's grace to others? How can I learn to trust that the living water flows not through my effort, but through Christ's sufficiency?

Prayer: God of mercy, meet me in my weariness. When I strike instead of speak, let your grace still flow. Teach me to trust your holiness more than my strength, and to lead not through striving, but through surrender. Amen.

Day 30: When Mountains Become Altars

Reading: Numbers 20:14–29

The wilderness winds on. Dust clings to sandals, grief clings to hearts. Miriam is gone, the people are restless, and the path ahead grows steep. Now comes another heartbreak, one both political and personal.

Moses sends envoys to the king of Edom, asking for safe passage through his land. His message is humble, almost pleading: "We're your relatives . . . please let us pass through your country. We won't turn aside to field or vineyard, nor drink water from any well." It's a reasonable request, a family appeal. Edom and Israel share a common ancestry through Esau and Jacob. But the answer comes back hard: "You mustn't pass through." And when Moses persists, Edom marches out with force to block the way.

The people turn aside. No battle. No retaliation. Just another road of disappointment.

It's a moment of unspectacular defeat, one easily overlooked. But here, God teaches something that power rarely understands: not every closed door is failure. Sometimes, holiness looks like restraint. Israel's journey is shaped not only by conquest but by surrender: by the long obedience that trusts God even when dignity is denied.

Then comes the second blow. God tells Moses and Aaron that the time has come for Aaron to die. The wilderness has been full of rebellion and loss, but this one cuts deeper. Aaron isn't a nameless elder; he's the brother who stood beside Moses before Pharaoh, who carried the rod that split the Nile and stretched over the Red Sea. He's the first high priest, the one who bore the names of Israel over his heart.

Now, he'll climb Mount Hor and lay it all down.

Moses, Aaron, and Eleazar ascend together. At the summit, Moses removes Aaron's priestly garments and places them on Eleazar, his son. It's a sacred unrobing, a liturgy of loss. The vestments that once glittered with divine calling are passed to another. Aaron dies there, on the mountain, in the presence of the one he served beside and the son who will carry the mantle.

When Moses and Eleazar descend, the people mourn for thirty days. For once, there's no rebellion, no complaint, only shared grief. The wilderness pauses.

This passage humbles every notion of leadership built on permanence or power. Even the greatest servants of God must hand over what they love. True faith learns to release with reverence: to let go of role, recognition, and control, trusting that God's work continues beyond our season. The mountain of Aaron's death becomes an altar where faithfulness is measured not by how long we lead, but by how well we finish.

In the end, this story turns our eyes to another mountain. Centuries later, Christ will ascend not with priestly robes, but with a cross upon his shoulders. He, too, will lay down his life for the people, and through that surrender, the priesthood will never end.

The wilderness teaches us this: every ending in God's story is a seed of a new beginning.

Guiding Truth: Holiness isn't only found in victories, but in the grace to surrender what we love and trust God with the future.

Reflection: What might God be asking me to release with open hands: some role, dream, or identity I've clung to for too long? How can I honor the faithfulness of those who've gone before me, carrying their mantle with humility and gratitude?

Prayer: God of holy endings, teach me to release what's not mine to keep. Let every mountain of loss become an altar of trust. When I pass on what I've been given, may your glory remain, and may your story continue through those who follow. Amen.

Day 31: The Serpent Lifted High

Reading: Numbers 21:1–9

The wilderness is beginning to wear thin on the people of God. Decades of wandering have worn away their patience, dimmed their hope, and exposed the cracks in their trust. Though victories have begun (Arad defeated, the Canaanites subdued), their spirits remain fragile. The road ahead twists through desert valleys, and discouragement seeps in like dust through their sandals.

Then, once again, the familiar pattern returns: "They spoke against God and against Moses, saying, 'Why have you brought us up out of Egypt to die in the wilderness? There's no bread! There's no water! And we detest this miserable food!'"

It's a tragic refrain: forgetting grace in the face of discomfort, despising manna even as it sustains them. In response, God sends venomous snakes among the people. Their bites bring death, their presence terror. The wilderness becomes a place of poison. The people cry out, confessing their sin, begging Moses to intercede.

God answers, but not in the way anyone expects. There's no removal of snakes, no instant deliverance. Instead, God tells Moses: "Make a serpent and put it on a pole; anyone who is bitten can look at it and live."

Moses obeys. He fashions a bronze serpent and lifts it high above the camp. Those who look upon it are healed. The poison remains real, but so does the power to overcome it.

It's one of the most haunting images in Scripture: healing that comes through looking directly at the source of pain. God doesn't erase the consequence; God transforms it. The very symbol of judgment becomes the instrument of mercy. To be saved, the people must look: not away, but at the thing that terrifies them.

Here, the wilderness reveals a profound spiritual truth. Transformation doesn't come by denial or avoidance. It comes through honest encounter: facing what's broken and trusting God to bring life from death. The bronze serpent is a paradox of grace: what once killed now heals. The instrument of death becomes a channel of divine compassion.

Centuries later, Jesus will recall this story when speaking to Nicodemus: "Just as Moses lifted up the serpent in the wilderness, so must the Son of Man be lifted up, that everyone who believes may have eternal life." The cross becomes the ultimate fulfillment of this strange symbol. Humanity's violence, pride, and sin (our venom) are lifted onto the wood. And there, God turns judgment into salvation.

To look upon the crucified Christ is to face what our sin has done and to discover, to our astonishment, that love is stronger than poison.

We still live in a world full of serpents: systems that wound, words that poison, fears that paralyze. But God's healing still comes through the same invitation: Look and live.

Guiding Truth: God heals not by erasing pain, but by transforming it: turning what wounds into what saves.

Reflection: What poison (fear, bitterness, shame) am I being invited to face in God's light rather than hide from? How might looking honestly at the cross bring healing to places in me that have long been numb or afraid?

Prayer: Merciful God, lift my eyes to the cross. Help me face the things I fear to see and find your mercy waiting there. Turn the poison of my sin into the healing of your grace, that I may live, restored and made whole. Amen.

Day 32: The Song of the Well

Reading: Numbers 21:10–20

The wilderness has been long and unforgiving. The people have grumbled, fought, mourned, and buried more than they can count. Yet in this stretch of Numbers 21, the story shifts from venom and death to movement and song. The rhythm changes. The people are no longer paralyzed by fear or regret; they're walking forward again.

The passage reads like a travel log: they journey from Oboth to Iye Abarim, then to the valley of Zered, onward to Arnon, tracing the edge of Moab. It's a geography of grace: dry ground slowly giving way to water and hope. After years of circling, they are finally moving toward promise. But what matters here isn't just where they go, it's what happens along the way.

At a place called Beer ("well"), God says to Moses, "Gather the people together and I'll give them water." It's a familiar promise. But this time, there's no murmuring, no striking the rock, no rebellion. The people don't demand; they sing. "Spring up, O well! Sing to it!"

This is the first recorded song of joy in the wilderness since the shores of the Red Sea. Back then, they sang because they had seen deliverance. Here, they sing before the water even rises. It's a song of trust, a melody born not from victory but from faith.

The well becomes a sacred symbol, not just of physical provision but of spiritual renewal. The leaders dig with staves, the people sing, and God provides. It's a partnership of divine grace and human response, a rhythm of faith that flows from participation, not passivity.

In a world that often demands certainty before celebration, this moment teaches a deeper kind of worship. To sing to the well before it springs is to trust that God's promise holds even in unseen depths. Faith, in its purest form, is often anticipatory praise: the courage to rejoice while the ground still looks dry.

This brief, often overlooked section of Numbers marks a pivotal turning point in the wilderness narrative. Israel begins to recover its voice. The community moves from lament to hope, from survival to song. The desert hasn't disappeared, but the people have rediscovered their God in it. The wilderness remains, yet something has changed within them.

And this well (like so many in Scripture) points beyond itself. It foreshadows the living water Jesus would later promise: "The water I give will become in them a spring of water welling up to eternal life." The same Spirit that turned the desert into a well now turns human hearts into fountains of grace.

Every wilderness season eventually reaches this place: a moment where faith must learn to sing before it sees.

Guiding Truth: Faith learns to sing to the well before the water flows, trusting that God's promise runs deeper than the desert.

Reflection: Where in my life is God asking me to sing in expectation rather than wait for proof? How might I recover joy as an act of faith in a world parched by cynicism and fear?

Prayer: God of the living well, teach me to sing in dry places. Let my praise draw water from the depths of your promise. When the desert stretches long, remind me that your presence flows beneath the surface, waiting to rise in due time. Amen.

Day 33: Learning to Fight by Faith

Reading: Numbers 21:21–35

The people of Israel are no longer wandering aimlessly. Something has changed. The desert has taught them trust, the well has taught them joy, and now they must learn courage. After years of delay and disobedience, they begin to walk into the promise again: not by avoiding conflict, but by entering it faithfully.

The passage begins with diplomacy. Israel sends messengers to Sihon, king of the Amorites, asking permission to pass peacefully through his land. It's the same appeal they made to Edom, the same humble offer: "We won't turn aside into field or vineyard; we won't drink from your wells." But once again, the answer is no. Sihon refuses passage and instead gathers his army to attack.

This time, however, there's no retreat. Israel meets the Amorites in battle, and with divine help, they prevail. The text says: "Israel defeated him with the sword and took possession of his land." From there, they settle in the captured towns and continue forward, defeating Og, king of Bashan, as well. What appears to be a military victory is, in truth, a spiritual milestone.

The generation that once trembled before giants has learned to stand. The people who once longed for Egypt now trust that God's presence goes before them. The God who provided water from the rock now gives strength for resistance. This isn't triumphalism; it's faith turned outward, obedience lived in motion.

These battles aren't about conquest for its own sake. They're about reclaiming the vocation of a people formed to bless the world. The land matters not as territory, but as testimony. Every victory declares that God's faithfulness is stronger than fear, and that human delay doesn't undo divine promise.

And yet, the story also humbles us. For Israel, every battle will later tempt pride; every victory will carry the risk of forgetting. But for now, in this moment, the people are walking in alignment. Their courage is born of remembered mercy. The wilderness has done its work; it's stripped them of illusion and taught them dependence.

We, too, are called to these battles, though ours may not be fought with swords. We face the empires of greed, fear, apathy, and despair that still wound the world. To follow the God of Israel is to resist these powers: not by domination, but through faith, justice, and love. Every act of courage, every stand for truth, becomes a way of participating in God's restoration.

This passage ends with a reminder: "So Israel settled in the land of the Amorites." The word "settled" is gentle, almost understated. But for a people who have lived for decades in tents, it is a whisper of fulfillment. Promise is becoming reality. Faith has found its footing.

They sang to the well; now they walk in victory. The same Spirit that taught them to trust still teaches us to fight: not for conquest, but for the peaceable, just, holy, loving, inclusive kingdom.

Guiding Truth: The God who brings water from rock also gives courage for the battle: faith becomes real when it moves from song to struggle.

Reflection: Where might God be calling me to step into challenge or confrontation, trusting divine strength more than self-sufficiency? How can my resistance to injustice or despair be rooted not in anger, but in worshipful trust?

Prayer: God of courage and compassion, teach me to fight by faith. Let your Spirit be my strength and your promise my purpose. In every battle I face, within and without, remind me that victory belongs to your mercy, not my might. Amen.

Day 34: When Donkeys See What Prophets Miss

Reading: Numbers 22:1–40

The story shifts now from the wilderness to the borderlands, from Israel's inner struggles to the fearful gaze of their neighbors. The Israelites camp on the plains of Moab, overlooking Jericho. Word spreads quickly: stories of victories over Sihon and Og, whispers of a God who fights for this strange, wandering people. King Balak of Moab trembles. He's seen what power can't stop. So he turns to something darker: he sends for Balaam, a pagan seer known for his curses and blessings.

"Come," Balak pleads, "curse these people for me, for they're too powerful for me." He's desperate to control what he fears, to harness the divine for his own ends. Religion becomes weaponized: a tool of empire, not worship.

Balaam's story unfolds with irony so thick it borders on satire. At first, he seems pious. He tells Balak's messengers, "I'll only speak what the Lord tells me." But as more envoys come bearing greater rewards, greed seeps through his restraint. Balaam is torn between obedience and opportunity, between reverence and reward. God tells him not to go, but he asks again, hoping perhaps for a different answer.

Then comes one of Scripture's strangest and most revealing scenes. Balaam mounts his donkey and sets out, but God's anger burns. An angel stands in the road, sword drawn, unseen by Balaam but visible to his donkey. Three times the animal swerves: into a field, against a wall, and finally collapses beneath him. Each time Balaam strikes her. And then the absurd happens: "Then the Lord opened the donkey's mouth, and she said to Balaam, 'What have I done to make you beat me these three times?'"

It's almost comic, yet painfully sharp. The prophet, revered for hearing divine mysteries, can't see what a donkey perceives. The animal's voice exposes Balaam's blindness. When his eyes are finally opened, he falls to the ground before the angel and confesses, "I've sinned."

The story is dripping with paradox. A pagan seer speaks truth. A donkey becomes a prophet. God uses irony to humble the wise and mercy to redirect the misguided. Balaam's vision is restored, but the lesson lingers: revelation belongs not to status or power, but to those with eyes to see and hearts to yield.

This passage unmasks the arrogance that can corrupt even spiritual work: the temptation to use God rather than be used by God. Balaam's donkey reminds us that our worthiness doesn't limit divine truth. God can speak through anything: a stranger, a child, even a creature of burden. Holiness often hides in places the proud overlook.

The real miracle here isn't a talking donkey, but a God who refuses to abandon the spiritually blind. Balaam's journey serves as a mirror for us, warning against manipulating faith for personal gain and inviting us to listen for God's voice in unexpected places.

Guiding Truth: God's voice can't be bought, contained, or controlled: true vision begins in humility, not power.

Reflection: Where might I be using faith to serve my own interests rather than letting God redirect my heart? Who or what might be speaking truth to me from the margins: voices I've ignored or dismissed?

Prayer: God of surprising voices, open my eyes to see what I've missed. Silence my pride long enough to hear your truth, even if it comes from unexpected lips. Make me humble enough to follow where you lead, and wise enough to stop when you stand in the road. Amen.

Day 35: You Can't Curse What God Has Blessed

Reading: Numbers 23:1–26

The plains of Moab shimmer beneath the sun. King Balak stands on a ridge, his eyes fixed on the vast camp of Israel spread across the desert like a sea of tents. His heart burns with fear and envy. Twice, he has summoned Balaam, the prophet-for-hire, to curse these people he can't defeat. Twice, God has warned Balaam not to speak anything but what God commands. Yet Balak, still clinging to the illusion of control, insists that with the proper ritual, the right vantage point, the correct words, he might bend divine power to his will.

So they build seven altars, offer bulls and rams, and stand waiting for magic to happen. Religion, stripped of faith, becomes performance: an attempt to control mystery rather than surrender to it. Balaam goes aside to "seek an oracle," and God meets him, not because Balaam is pure, but because God is faithful. The Spirit speaks through even a compromised mouth.

Balaam returns and delivers the first oracle. His words ring out across the desert air: "How can I curse those whom God has not cursed? How can I denounce those whom the Lord hasn't denounced?"

In one sentence, every ambition of Balak collapses. The sheer sovereignty of God undermines the king's desire to manipulate blessings into curses. What God blesses remains blessed. What God chooses can't be undone by fear, hatred, or politics.

Then Balaam declares something more profound, something astonishing even to himself: "From the top of the crags I see them . . . a people who live apart and don't consider themselves one of the nations." Israel's distinction is a divine calling. God means them to embody another kind of life: a community defined not by empire or domination, but by holiness and hope.

Balak is furious. He demands that Balaam try again from another location, as if divine truth depends on geography or angle. But when Balaam seeks God again, the same answer comes: blessing. Always blessing. "God isn't human, that God should lie, or a mortal, that God should change God's mind. Has God spoken, and will God not act?"

It's one of the most profound affirmations of divine integrity in all Scripture. God isn't fickle or bribable. The holy word isn't subject to political mood or emotional whim. Divine blessing doesn't shift with circumstance; it stands, because it flows from the very heart of steadfast love. Balak wants control. Balaam wants profit. But God wants truth, and truth wins.

This story reverberates through time. Still today, power tries to weaponize religion, to pronounce curses upon those who threaten its comfort. But the word of the Lord stands firm: "You can't curse what I've blessed."

God's blessing rests not on perfection but on promise. It's a covenant, not a performance. And when God speaks life, no empire, no scheme, no fear can unmake it.

Guiding Truth: No power can curse what God has blessed; divine truth cannot be manipulated or contained.

Reflection: Where have I tried to control outcomes rather than trust the unchanging goodness of God's word? Who in my world is being cursed by systems or voices that God has already blessed, and how can I speak blessing instead?

Prayer: God of unbreakable promise, silence the voices of fear and manipulation around me. Teach me to trust your blessing even when others speak against it. Let my words echo your faithfulness, and my life bear witness that your truth can't be undone. Amen.

Day 36: The Unstoppable Blessing

Reading: Numbers 24:1–25

Balaam stands on a mountain, looking down on Israel's tents: orderly, peaceful, radiant beneath the desert sun. Three times he's tried to curse them. Three times God has overturned the curse into a blessing. By the fourth, Balaam knows better. The text says he "didn't seek omens as before," but turned his face toward the wilderness, and the Spirit of God came upon him. Out of that vision pours a word not of judgment but of breathtaking grace: "How beautiful are your tents, O Jacob, your dwellings, O Israel." What began as manipulation becomes revelation. The hired prophet finds himself caught up in a truth he can't control: the blessing of God is unstoppable.

This passage is the climax of a long story of spiritual blindness and reluctant obedience. Balaam had one foot in the world of greed and another in the world of prophecy. But when he finally releases control (when he stops trying to conjure outcomes), he sees clearly. He sees what God sees: a people chosen not for their perfection but for grace's purpose. His blessing turns prophetic: "A star shall come out of Jacob, a scepter shall rise out of Israel." That star points forward to Jesus Christ, the light breaking through human shadow, the one who blesses where the world curses, who reigns by mercy, not might.

This moment echoes Luke 11:1–13, where Jesus teaches the disciples to pray, "Your kingdom come." Both Balaam and the disciples learn that prayer and prophecy begin where control ends. Balaam stopped seeking omens; Jesus told his followers to stop grasping, to ask and trust instead. God gives not stones but bread, not serpents but fish, not illusions but the Holy Spirit. The movement from manipulation to surrender is the heartbeat of authentic spirituality.

For us, this story is a mirror. We often stand where Balaam stood, trying to bend the divine will toward our desires. We pray to win rather than to yield, to preserve rather than to transform. Yet the Spirit still comes when we turn our face toward the wilderness, toward the unknown terrain where God's promise outstrips our plans. There, we discover that blessing isn't earned or engineered; it's received. And once received, it must flow outward to fellow believers, neighbors, strangers, and even enemies.

Balaam's vision reveals a God who blesses those the world despises, who turns curses into instruments of redemption. That's the character of the Holy One. So, our vocation is clear: to speak blessing where others sow bitterness, to trust divine generosity over human anxiety, to participate in a grace that can't be bought or sold.

Through Jesus, the true Star of Jacob, the curse has been undone. The wilderness becomes a place of light. Every prayer that begins with surrender ends in praise.

Guiding Truth: Turn your face toward the wilderness and trust the Spirit who transforms curses into blessings.

Reflection: Where am I still trying to manipulate God's will rather than surrender to it? What would it mean for me to bless rather than curse those who oppose me?

Prayer: God of mercy, teach me to release control and receive your blessing. Where I see barrenness, let your light arise. Make my words instruments of grace, my heart a dwelling of peace, and my life a witness to the unstoppable power of your love. Amen.

Day 37: Zeal, Idolatry, and the Wounds of Love

Reading: Numbers 25:1–18

The story of Numbers 25 is raw and unsettling. Israel, poised at the threshold of the promised land, falters again. Seduced by the Moabites and their gods, they feast and bow down before Baal of Peor. The people who were called to bear divine blessing to the nations are instead absorbed by the very patterns they were meant to heal. Their worship turns into self-indulgence; covenant becomes compromise.

The text unfolds like a moral earthquake. God's anger burns, not because of fragile pride, but because love refuses to coexist with the idolatry that destroys souls. In the chaos, Phinehas steps forward. With a single act of zeal, he halts the plague consuming Israel. The story ends with a strange and fierce mercy: "He was jealous with my jealousy," God says, "and I give him my covenant of peace."

This passage is difficult to stomach, especially in a culture that is suspicious of passion or absolutes. But beneath its violence lies a more profound truth. Love that doesn't resist evil isn't love at all. Divine zeal isn't rage; it's holy compassion that refuses to let death have the last word. The plague that swept through the camp mirrors the moral infection of idolatry, the soul's surrender to false loves that promise intimacy but breed decay.

The connection to Luke 11:1–13 sheds light on this matter. Jesus teaches that prayer is persistent, trusting, and rooted in the goodness of

God. The contrast is striking: Israel in Numbers 25 turns to idols for provision; Jesus calls us to ask the true Father for daily bread. One path seeks satisfaction through control; the other opens empty hands in trust. The lesson is timeless: where prayer is absent, idolatry rushes in.

Spiritually, this text confronts us with uncomfortable honesty. We may not bow before carved idols, but we often offer our hearts to the gods of comfort, productivity, reputation, or romance. We seek belonging without holiness, intimacy without covenant, success without service. Yet the Spirit's jealousy is the fierce longing of divine love to restore integrity, to draw us back into wholeness.

In Jesus Christ, the zeal of God finds its ultimate form, not in the spear of Phinehas but in the cross. There, divine holiness and mercy meet. Christ's body absorbs the plague of sin; the spear pierces not the guilty but the innocent. Through his wound, peace flows. What was once judgment becomes reconciliation. The "covenant of peace" given to Phinehas is fulfilled in the crucified one who breaks the power of false worship and calls us to love that is pure, courageous, and free.

To follow this Christ is to live with holy passion: for justice that restores, for mercy that costs, for love that purifies. It means naming our idols, turning again to the one who alone satisfies.

Guiding Truth: True zeal is love's fierce courage: the passion to tear down idols so peace may dwell within and among us.

Reflection: What idols still capture my loyalty or imagination more than God's love? How can holy passion express itself through compassion, justice, and forgiveness today?

Prayer: Holy One, cleanse my heart of divided loves. Teach me zeal that heals, not harms; passion that builds peace, not pride. Through Jesus, the true bearer of your covenant, make me a vessel of your reconciling love in a fractured world. Amen.

Day 38: Counting What Endures

Reading: Numbers 26:1–65

After the devastation of idolatry and plague, God commands Moses and Eleazar to take a census: a count dedicated to showing God's goodness and promise. A generation has perished in the wilderness; a new one stands ready to enter the land. The names are read, tribe by tribe, family by family. Each number represents a story, a lineage, a life touched by both failure and grace. What began with rebellion ends with renewal. The numbering is benediction. It declares that even in the aftermath of sin, God still counts, still remembers, still calls a people forward.

At first glance, this chapter appears to be a ledger of statistics. But hidden within it is a theology of remembrance. Every number is an act of grace. The wilderness had been a graveyard of dreams, yet here, God gathers the living, numbering them for inheritance. To count is to affirm worth. No one is forgotten. The divine promise didn't die in the desert; it simply awaited resurrection.

Spiritually, this passage reminds us that faithfulness often looks like slow rebuilding after loss. We want miracles that erase failure; God offers mercy that redeems it. This census follows the wreckage of betrayal, yet it announces hope: a new generation will see what their parents only glimpsed. It's a story about continuity through grace. When everything seems fractured, God reconstitutes a people, teaching them to trust again.

This is where Luke 11:1–13 enters the story. Jesus teaches his disciples to pray, "Give us today our daily bread." The same God who numbered Israel's tribes still counts our days and provides what's needed for each of us. We live, not by possession, but by providence. The census tells us we belong to a God who knows us by name; the prayer teaches us to depend daily on that knowing.

Theologically, Numbers 26 reveals divine patience. God works through generations, not moments. When one falters, another rises. When a community falls into despair, God gathers what remains and breathes new purpose into it. In our own times (when institutions decline, faith seems fragile, and the future feels uncertain), this chapter whispers courage: the promise still stands. God is still counting. God's covenant still holds.

This text calls us to live with the quiet steadfastness of those who believe that every act of faith, every prayer whispered in the wilderness, every gesture of kindness, adds to the number of those who inherit life. To follow Jesus is to trust that no moment of faithfulness is wasted. He is the fulfillment of the census: the one in whom every tribe and nation finds belonging, the shepherd who knows each sheep by name, the redeemer who counts even the hairs on our heads.

Guiding Truth: God's love counts what the world forgets: every life, every act of faith, every small beginning of renewal.

Reflection: Where do I need to let God re-count and re-claim what feels lost in me? How can I embody the patient hope that rebuilds faith and community after failure?

Prayer: God of remembrance, you number stars and souls alike. Count me among those who trust your promise. Where I've grown weary, renew my courage; where I've been forgotten, remind me I'm known. Teach me to see each life as sacred and each day as a gift of grace. Amen.

Day 39: The Daughters Who Dared to Ask

Reading: Numbers 27:1–11

In a story often buried beneath the wars and wanderings of Israel, five women step into sacred history. Mahlah, Noah, Hoglah, Milcah, and Tirzah (the daughters of Zelophehad) stand before Moses, Eleazar, the chiefs, and the entire assembly. Their father has died in the wilderness, leaving no sons. The law, as it stood, excluded them from inheritance. But they speak up: "Why should our father's name disappear from his clan because he had no son? Give us a portion among our father's relatives." Their words echo like prophecy, daring to question injustice not with rebellion but with faith.

Moses listens, then brings their case before God. The divine answer is startling in its simplicity and grace: "The daughters of Zelophehad are right." With those words, a new precedent is born. Justice expands. Inheritance is extended. God's command is rewritten to include those previously left out. It's a revolution in the wilderness: a revelation that the covenant's boundaries are more elastic, merciful, and inclusive than human structures often imagine.

This story is about trust. The daughters appeal to divine righteousness. They act not from arrogance but from the conviction that God's promises must be true for all of God's people. In doing so, they embody the kind of faith Jesus later describes in Luke 11:1–13— persistent, courageous, and expectant. Like those who ask for bread and trust that God won't hand them a stone, these women ask for justice and find mercy. They show us that prayer is the bold articulation of trust in God's fairness.

Spiritually, this passage calls us to believe that divine justice doesn't shrink; it unfolds. The God who heard these women's plea still listens to voices long ignored or dismissed. When we speak up for inclusion, equity, and dignity, we echo their faith. To follow Jesus is to walk in this same spirit of courageous trust; to believe that God's kingdom is large enough to hold every life, every story, every inheritance of grace.

The daughters of Zelophehad didn't just change a law; they revealed a truth about God's heart. The covenant is a widening embrace. Their faith anticipates the Christ who opens the kingdom to the marginalized, who welcomes the overlooked, who says, "Ask, and it'll be given to you."

This text becomes a summons: to pray boldly, to act justly, and to believe that God's love is expansive enough to restore what has been denied. The daughters dared to ask, and heaven answered.

Guiding Truth: Faith asks boldly for the justice that love demands and trusts God to widen the circle of grace.

Reflection: Where might I be called to ask for justice or inclusion, not only for myself but for others? How does my prayer life reflect the daughters' courageous faith in God's fairness?

Prayer: God of mercy and truth, teach me to speak when silence would protect injustice. Give me faith that trusts your goodness enough to ask boldly. Widen my heart to see your grace embracing all who call upon your name. Amen.

Day 40: Passing the Mantle

Reading: Numbers 27:12–23

The mountain breeze is sharp as Moses stands upon Nebo's heights. From there, God shows him the promised land: Canaan stretching like a dream across the horizon. He will see it but not enter it. The weight of years and mercy, of failure and faithfulness, settles on his shoulders. Moses, the friend of God, the liberator and lawgiver, now faces the twilight of his calling. Yet his last act isn't lament; it's care. He turns his attention to the future of the people he loves.

When Moses pleads, "May the Lord, the God of the spirits of all flesh, appoint someone over this community," his concern is shepherding, not legacy. He asks for a leader who will "go out before them and come in before them, one who will lead them out and bring them in." Leadership, in this prayer, is companionship: guidance born of presence. And God answers: "Take Joshua, son of Nun, a person in whom is the Spirit."

The story unfolds like a sacred handover. Moses lays his hands on Joshua before the priest and the whole assembly. Authority passes not through lineage or ambition, but through Spirit-filled humility. It's an act of trust in both God and community: a visible sign that the mission belongs not to a single hero but to a living people guided by grace.

This moment resonates with Jesus' teaching on prayer in Luke 11:1–13. Just as the disciples ask how to pray and Jesus responds by teaching them to depend on the Father's goodness, so Moses asks for provision: not bread this time, but a shepherd. Both prayers reveal that divine generosity meets human need not with scarcity but with sufficiency. God gives not stones but the Spirit, not substitutes but successors.

Spiritually, this text speaks to all who struggle with transition: with letting go, with entrusting what we've built to another's care. In Moses' obedience, we see a deep surrender. He accepts that his vocation was never ownership but stewardship. His life's work culminates not in crossing the Jordan, but in preparing another to do so. Such humility is rare and holy. It reminds us that the story of faith is larger than our part in it.

Through Jesus, this passage gains even more profound meaning. The laying on of hands points toward the pattern of discipleship and commissioning that continues in the church. Each generation receives what another has carried: the Spirit of wisdom, the calling to serve, the vision of a kingdom yet to be fully entered. The work is never finished, yet it's never without hope.

To live this way is to see leadership as love in motion: to bless the next person, to trust the Spirit, to release the future into hands not our own.

Guiding Truth: Authentic leadership relinquishes control, trusting the Spirit to carry out God's work through others.

Reflection: What am I being asked to release so that God's work can continue beyond me? How can I nurture others to lead with humility, courage, and Spirit-filled wisdom?

Prayer: God of all generations, teach me the grace of release. Let me lead by blessing, not grasping. Fill those who follow with your Spirit's wisdom and strength. May every act of handing over become a sign of your faithfulness from age to age. Amen.

Day 41: The Rhythm of Daily Offering

Reading: Numbers 28:1–10

After chapters of rebellion, renewal, and transition, the story turns to worship. God instructs Moses about the daily offerings: two lambs, one in the morning and one at twilight, with grain and drink poured out as accompaniment. It's a simple pattern, repeated every day, every year, across generations. Nothing dramatic, nothing dazzling, just the steady rhythm of devotion.

At first glance, this passage might seem a pause between grander stories, but it's the heartbeat of the covenant. The daily offering (morning and evening) reminds Israel that life is lived before the face of God, framed by gratitude and surrender. Each dawn begins with remembrance; each dusk ends with trust. The people's sacrifices don't manipulate the divine or earn favor. They rehearse dependence. They sanctify ordinary time.

In a world addicted to spectacle and constant motion, this text invites us to rediscover the holiness of rhythm. Worship isn't meant to be a rare event but a daily posture. The morning lamb and evening lamb teach us that faith matures not through great bursts of zeal, but through constancy; through showing up in love day after day, even when the heart feels barren.

Jesus echoes this rhythm in Luke 11:1–13, where he teaches his followers to pray, "Give us each day our daily bread." The same spirit breathes through both texts. In Numbers 28, God feeds the divine-human relationship through daily offerings; in Luke, Jesus teaches us to feed our souls through daily trust. Faith isn't a weekly spectacle but a daily bread kind of thing: regular, sustaining, unhurried. The offerings and the prayers both embody gratitude and surrender: what we have, we give; what we need, we receive.

Spiritually, this passage challenges our modern disconnection from sacred routine. Many of us live scattered lives: fragmented, hurried, exhausted. The invitation here is to re-establish sacred rhythm: morning and evening prayer, moments of reflection, simple rituals of attention that turn our gaze back to God. These are not relics of ancient religion; they're anchors for weary hearts.

The lamb offered each day points forward to Christ, the Lamb once offered for all. His life fulfills the rhythm of sacrifice; his presence transforms ritual into relationship. Yet even with that fulfillment, the pattern remains: we still rise and rest, still offer our hearts in gratitude and trust. Christ's grace doesn't abolish the rhythm; it deepens it. Our daily prayers and acts of love become living offerings, not to appease God, but to align with divine love.

The daily offering reminds us that holiness grows quietly through repetition, faithfulness, and the unseen places of devotion.

Guiding Truth: Let your days be framed by gratitude and surrender: morning and evening offerings of trust to the God who provides.

Reflection: What daily practices help me stay aware of God's presence and rely on divine grace? How can I turn ordinary routines into sacred rhythms of worship?

Prayer: Eternal One, teach me to meet you in the quiet rhythms of my days. May my mornings begin with praise and my evenings rest in trust. Receive the small offerings of my heart, and make them fragrant with your peace. Amen.

Day 42: The Calendar of Holiness

Reading: Numbers 28:11–29:11

The divine instructions continue, unfolding into a sacred rhythm of time. From the daily offerings (Numbers 28:1–10), the text moves outward: to the new moons, the feasts, the Passover, the Festival of Weeks, the seventh month, and the Day of Atonement. Each season, at its appointed time, holds its own offerings: bulls, rams, lambs, grain, oil, and wine. The list is long and precise, but beneath its detail beats a simple truth: God orders time around communion. The holy calendar isn't about appeasement but remembrance, gratitude, and renewal.

To the ancient Israelites, these sacrifices wove meaning into the year. They marked time as sacred, transforming the ordinary march of days into a living liturgy. Every festival recalled divine faithfulness; every new moon declared that even the cycles of nature belonged to God. This was a theology of time itself: an invitation to live not as captives to hours and seasons, but as participants in grace that renews creation.

The rituals were demanding. Bulls and rams, oil and wine, every measure carefully prescribed. Yet this detail reveals not the burden of religion but the attentiveness of love. Devotion is found not only in great emotion but in careful obedience. These festivals taught Israel to live rhythmically, allowing gratitude, rest, repentance, and joy to shape their community.

When Jesus teaches his disciples to pray in Luke 11:1–13, he speaks from within this world of rhythm. His words ("Your kingdom come, your will be done," and "Give us each day our daily bread") reimagine the festival heart of Israel for the life of the Spirit. The yearly sacrifices become daily surrender. The fixed calendar becomes the continual offering of one's heart. In Christ, the feast days are fulfilled: not abolished but transfigured. He becomes both the center and the content of the calendar.

For us, this passage speaks powerfully into a culture that treats time as a commodity. We schedule ourselves to the point of exhaustion and call it productivity. But sacred time resists that tyranny. It teaches us that life isn't to be managed but received. The holy days were God's way of slowing the people down: calling them back to remembrance, dependence, and delight.

In Christ, every day becomes holy ground. We no longer need bulls or rams, yet the invitation remains: mark your days by grace. Celebrate divine generosity. Rest in divine mercy. Repent, feast, remember. Let your life be a calendar of gratitude, where work, rest, lament, and joy each find their appointed time before God.

The festivals of Numbers 28–29 look forward to the true Feast: the kingdom Jesus inaugurates, where time itself is healed and all creation joins the song of renewal. Until then, we keep time by love and faithfulness, offering each season and each breath back to the One who sanctifies them.

Guiding Truth: Let your time be shaped by grace: each day, season, and year offered back to the One who fills it with meaning.

Reflection: How do I mark time: by anxiety, ambition, or gratitude and grace? What rhythms, seasons, or practices could help me live more consciously in God's time?

Prayer: God of days and seasons, teach me to keep time as you do. Fill my calendar with your presence. May my work, rest, and worship all flow from gratitude, and may every season of my life become an offering of love to you. Amen.

Day 43: The Festival of Joyful Surrender

Reading: Numbers 29:12–40

The passage describes the final sequence of offerings for Israel's year, culminating in the seven days of the Festival of Booths (Sukkot) and the solemn gathering on the eighth day. The text lists offerings with precision: thirteen bulls the first day, twelve the next, then eleven, ten, down to seven: seventy in all. Grain, oil, and drink accompany each, as if the whole earth is being poured out before God. It's repetitive, rhythmic, and extravagant. Yet beneath the arithmetic lies poetry: the slow diminuendo of sacrifice, a symphony of devotion marking the fullness of divine provision and human gratitude.

This festival was a celebration of harvest and of divine presence in the wilderness. Israel built temporary shelters, remembering their dependence on God's sheltering care. The booths reminded them: You were once wanderers, and it was grace that kept you alive. The offerings became acts of thanksgiving for abundance and confession of trust for the year ahead. The sheer scale of the sacrifices said, "Everything we have belongs to you."

Spiritually, this passage invites us to rediscover the joy of surrender. True worship is not minimalistic (giving just enough to satisfy obligation) but lavish, flowing from gratitude. When the heart knows it has been sustained by mercy, it gives freely. The decreasing number of bulls each day hints at this deeper rhythm: the movement from abundance to simplicity, from excess to intimacy. As the festival progresses, the noise of offering becomes quieter, the focus clearer. By the final day, what remains is presence.

Jesus embodies this final day. In the Gospel of John, during the same Feast of Booths, he stands and cries, "Let anyone thirsty come to me and drink." What Numbers prefigures, Jesus fulfills. The sacrifices end in him. The wine and oil, the bulls and lambs, the booths and blessings: all find their completion in the living water of his Spirit. The worship that once revolved around altars now flows from hearts. The temple becomes humanity itself: ordinary lives made sacred by divine indwelling.

Luke 11:1–13 echoes this same truth. The God who once accepted offerings of grain and lambs now gives the greatest gift: the Holy Spirit. Prayer becomes participation in divine generosity, not negotiation. To live in Christ is to inhabit Sukkot perpetually: to dwell in the tent of God's mercy, receiving daily bread, daily presence, daily renewal.

This passage asks us: How will we mark our abundance? Will we hoard it or pour it out in gratitude? Will our lives be altars of scarcity or celebration? The Feast of Booths calls us to rejoice in what God has given, to live lightly in the world, to share freely, and to remember that joy is a form of trust.

Guiding Truth: Joyful surrender is the most authentic form of worship; it is gratitude that pours itself out in trust and love.

Reflection: How might I turn my abundance (time, resources, gifts) into offerings of joy and generosity? What does it mean for me to "dwell in the tent of God's mercy" amid life's uncertainties?

Prayer: God of harvest and home, teach me to rejoice in your goodness. Let gratitude overflow into generosity, and worship into daily trust. May my life become a festival of your grace: a dwelling of joy, simplicity, and love in your enduring presence. Amen.

Day 44: The Weight of Our Words

Reading: Numbers 30:1–16

In this passage, God gives Moses detailed instructions about vows: promises made to God. It may seem like an administrative sidebar between dramatic stories, but here the text turns to something profoundly personal: the integrity of speech. Vows were voluntary; no one was forced to make them. Yet once spoken, they carried weight. To make a promise before God was to align the lips and the heart, to let words become covenant.

In ancient Israel, vows symbolized devotion and dependence. A vow might accompany a moment of desperation or gratitude, a way of saying, "If you sustain me, I'll dedicate this part of my life to you." Numbers 30 shows divine concern for honesty, commitment, and relational trust. Broken vows don't simply violate rules; they fracture communion. The passage holds men and women accountable, while also addressing the social realities of the time, specifically how authority and responsibility intersected in households. Though culturally bound, its spiritual principle remains timeless: integrity matters to God.

To live truthfully is itself a form of worship. Words are not disposable. Speech shapes worlds, builds relationships, and expresses the unseen movement of the soul. God's attention to vows reminds us that language is holy. We live in a culture awash in casual promises: quick "I'll pray for yous," empty "I love yous," vague commitments without follow-through. Yet every word spoken before God and others has moral weight. Speech can either heal or deceive, create trust or corrode it.

Jesus deepens this teaching in his own ministry. He says, "Let your 'Yes' be yes, and your 'No' be no." In Luke 11:1–13, his model of prayer continues this same integrity: simple, sincere, and dependent. "Father, hallowed be your name." No bargaining, no empty rhetoric. Just the honest cry of a heart aligned with divine purposes. In prayer as in promises, God desires reality, not performance.

Spiritually, this passage calls us to a speech that reflects the truth of who we are in Christ. When we make commitments (to God, to others, to our own souls), we participate in covenantal life. Every vow, formal or informal, becomes an echo of the divine faithfulness that never fails. God's own Word became flesh, entering history not as abstract principle but as fulfilled promise. In Christ, truth takes on skin and breath.

To follow Jesus, then, is to let our words carry the fragrance of his faithfulness. Our speech should mirror his steadfast love: measured, trustworthy, compassionate. We keep our word not out of fear, but out of love for the One whose promises never fail.

Guiding Truth: Let your words be as faithful as the God who speaks life: promise only what love can sustain, and keep it.

Reflection: Where have my words overreached my integrity: promises made but not lived? How can my speech become more truthful, compassionate, and dependable in daily life?

Prayer: God of truth, teach me to speak with care and courage. May my words reflect your faithfulness and bring healing, not harm. Where I've spoken lightly, grant repentance; where I've been silent, give me courage to promise and keep. May my life echo your steadfast Word. Amen.

Day 45: The Battle Within and the Mercy Beyond

Reading: Numbers 31:1–54

This is one of Scripture's most troubling passages. God commands Israel to take vengeance on Midian for leading them into idolatry at Peor. The narrative that follows is violent: armies sent, enemies slain, plunder divided, survivors counted. It jars modern readers and wounds tender hearts. Yet to wrestle with such texts is itself a holy act. Scripture does not sanitize the complexity of faith, nor the brutality of history. It reveals both divine judgment and human limitation, and it invites us to seek God's deeper purposes through the dust of conflict.

The story begins with justice, not conquest. The Midianites had deliberately seduced Israel into spiritual betrayal; this war is described as divine judgment against that destructive idolatry. But even here, the cost is immense. When the fighting ends, Moses himself is grieved by the incomplete obedience of his troops. Later, the soldiers bring their spoils and gold before the tent of meeting, not as a display of self-congratulation, but as an act of atonement, purification, and repentance for the bloodshed they have witnessed. The closing verses are unexpectedly tender: gratitude replaces triumph. "We have not lost one," they say. Their offering is an act of remembrance and humility.

Beneath the battle's surface lies a moral and spiritual truth: the real war is not against nations but against idolatry, deceit, and the corruption of the human heart. Israel's external war mirrors the interior one: our own struggle to root out the idols that twist love and deform community. The physical violence depicted in Numbers 31 is a shadow of the spiritual violence required to unmask evil and reclaim wholeness.

When we read this through the lens of Jesus Christ, everything shifts. The vengeance of Numbers becomes the victory of the cross. There, divine justice and mercy meet, not through killing, but through self-giving love. The battle is won by the Lamb who suffers, not the warrior who conquers. Christ absorbs wrath and ends the cycle of retribution. The gold of war becomes the treasure of grace. What the soldiers laid before the altar, we now lay before the cross: our sins, our pride, our need for control.

In Luke 11:1–13, Jesus teaches us to pray, "Forgive us our sins, for we also forgive everyone who sins against us." Here, the true battle is waged: not with swords, but with forgiveness. Prayer replaces vengeance; love disarms hostility. God's holiness, once expressed through fierce judgment, now shines in cruciform mercy.

This passage, uncomfortable as it is, calls us to face our own Midian: to confront what tempts us away from faithfulness. But it also invites us to lay down our weapons, to let Christ's peace complete the work of purification. The offerings of gold at the end of Numbers 31 prefigure our call to consecrate everything (our triumphs, wounds, and regrets) to God's healing grace.

Guiding Truth: The fiercest battles are within us, and they're won when we lay our weapons down before the mercy of Christ.

Reflection: What inner idols or resentments still wage war within me, and how might Christ's mercy disarm them? How can I turn vengeance into prayer and hostility into forgiveness in my relationships?

Prayer: God of mercy, teach me to lay down my sword. Purify my heart from anger, fear, and pride. Transform my battles into trust, my victories into gratitude. Through Jesus, the Lamb who conquers by love, make me an instrument of your peace. Amen.

Day 46: Settling Short of the Promise

Reading: Numbers 32:1–42

The tribes of Reuben and Gad stand before Moses with a practical request. They've seen the lush pastures east of the Jordan (land perfect for their herds), and they ask to settle there rather than cross into Canaan. On the surface, their reasoning makes sense: it's good land, they're herders, and they've already helped subdue it. But Moses hears something more profound: an echo of fear, of self-preservation, of the old wilderness hesitation. "Shall your brothers go to war while you sit here?" he asks, remembering the generation that refused to enter the land.

This story reveals a tension that resides in every soul: the temptation to settle for what's comfortable rather than trusting the fullness of God's promise. Reuben and Gad don't reject the covenant; they want to adjust it to fit their convenience. They want proximity to the promise without the cost of pilgrimage. And yet, to their credit, when Moses rebukes them, they repent. They promise to fight beside their kin until all the tribes receive their inheritance. Only then will they return east to their families. Moses agrees, and their words become a covenant.

Spiritually, this story is about compromise and faithfulness. The danger isn't always rebellion; sometimes it's settling. We find a pasture that meets our immediate needs and stop journeying toward the deeper life God intends. We trade calling for comfort, mission for maintenance. But God's vision is always larger than our convenience. Faith requires crossing the river: trusting that the unknown land ahead is where true life awaits.

And yet, there's grace in this story too. God allows Reuben, Gad, and half of Manasseh to settle east of the Jordan. The promise is not revoked. Divine mercy accommodates human frailty while still calling forth obedience. The covenant bends without breaking. God meets us where we are but never stops inviting us further in.

When read alongside Luke 11:1–13, the message sharpens. Jesus teaches us to pray, "Your kingdom come." It's a prayer of surrender, not settlement. It asks that God's reign extend into every territory of our lives: the ones we've conquered, and the ones we still fear to enter. To pray that prayer is to keep crossing rivers of trust. It's to believe that there's always more of God's promise waiting beyond our comfort zone.

In the end, Reuben and Gad do keep their word. They fight beside their siblings until the land is secured. Their faithfulness redeems their initial hesitation. It's a reminder that God honors integrity, even in the midst of compromise. The call is not to perfection, but to perseverance: to keep journeying toward unity, justice, and trust, wherever God leads.

Guiding Truth: Don't settle short of the promise: keep crossing the rivers of trust until love claims every part of your life.

Reflection: Where am I tempted to settle for comfort instead of continuing God's deeper journey in me? How might I keep faith with others: standing beside them until God's promises are fulfilled for all?

Prayer: God of promise and patience, keep me from settling for less than your call. When fear or comfort holds me back, please give me the courage to cross again. Teach me to walk in faith, to fight for others' good, and to trust that your promise is always worth the journey. Amen.

Day 47: Remembering the Journey

Reading: Numbers 33:1–49

This chapter reads like a travel log: forty-two stages of wandering, a litany of places whose names whisper stories: Rameses, Marah, Sinai, Kadesh, Mount Hor, the plains of Moab. Every campsite holds memory: miracles and murmuring, manna and rebellion, water from rock and graves in the sand. It's not a dramatic narrative, but a list: a geography of grace. Yet in this litany lies profound theology: God wanted the people to remember every step.

The journey from slavery to promise wasn't a straight line but a spiral through wilderness and wonder. By commanding Moses to record each place, God sanctifies the whole journey: the triumphs, failures, detours, and delays. Nothing is wasted. Every stop becomes part of the sacred story. The Israelites might have wanted to forget the wilderness, but God insists: remember. Not to romanticize suffering, but to recognize faithfulness. Divine presence was there: in the hard soil, in the long silences, in the unmarked miles.

Spiritually, this passage invites us to trace our own journey with similar honesty. Each of us has a map: seasons of bondage and freedom, dryness and discovery, disobedience and renewal. We're tempted to forget the painful parts, to skip ahead to the promised land. But remembering is itself an act of worship. It tells us that grace accompanied us even when we felt lost. Memory, sanctified by gratitude, becomes the soil of maturity.

This chapter also redefines progress. Israel covered vast terrain, yet the true movement wasn't measured in miles, but in the formation of the heart. The wilderness was God's school of trust. The record of campsites testifies that spiritual growth is rarely efficient: it's patient, meandering, and full of divine interruptions. The same Spirit who led them by cloud and fire still leads us through landscapes of uncertainty, teaching us to depend, to hope, to love.

In Luke 11:1–13, Jesus teaches his followers to pray with persistence: "Ask, seek, knock." That same persistence shaped Israel's wilderness years. Every stop was an answered prayer or a place where prayer had to be rediscovered. The list of locations is a mirror of our prayer life: seasons of clarity and confusion, petition and silence. Through it all, God remains constant, the faithful companion who neither abandons nor rushes us.

For Christians, this passage ultimately points to Christ: the one who walks with us through every stage of life's pilgrimage, who redeems our detours and transforms our failures into wisdom. The geography of grace now centers on him: every step, every loss, every dawn becomes part of the greater Exodus toward resurrection.

To remember is to awaken gratitude. To look back and see divine footprints beside our own is to find hope for the road ahead.

Guiding Truth: Remember where you've been: the wilderness, too, was holy ground where grace quietly kept you alive.

Reflection: What places or seasons of my journey have I tried to forget, and what hidden grace might still live there? How can remembering God's faithfulness in the past strengthen my trust for what's ahead?

Prayer: Faithful God, help me remember the long road and your quiet presence at every turn. Where I once saw only wandering, let me now see your mercy. Sanctify my story, redeem my detours, and lead me onward in gratitude and trust. Amen.

Day 48: The Call to Clear the Land

Reading: Numbers 33:50–56

As Israel stands on the brink of the promised land, God speaks with solemn clarity. The long wilderness journey is almost over; the Jordan lies before them like a line between memory and mission. But before they cross, God gives a warning: "When you enter the land of Canaan, you must drive out all its inhabitants, destroy their idols, demolish their high places, and take possession of the land." The command sounds severe, but its purpose is not conquest for conquest's sake: it's purification. The land is to be a sanctuary, free from the idols that enslave hearts.

This passage is about spiritual integrity, not territorial ambition. The call to "drive out" is a metaphor for holiness: an image of rooting out the forces that deform love and trust. Israel's danger isn't external enemies; it's internal compromise. The land is meant to be a place where worship flows unpolluted, where community mirrors divine justice and mercy. God knows that if the people allow idols to remain, they will slowly absorb their values (greed, cruelty, self-absorption) and the promised land will become another Egypt.

The warning in verses 55–56 is piercing: "If you do not drive out the inhabitants of the land, those you allow to remain will become barbs in your eyes and thorns in your sides." In other words, half-hearted obedience breeds future pain. Sin tolerated becomes sin enthroned. The idols we fail to confront end up shaping us. What Israel faced in Canaan, we face within: the call to clear the inner landscape of whatever keeps us from wholehearted trust in God.

Spiritually, this passage urges vigilance and surrender. God isn't asking for perfection but for devotion. The clearing of idols isn't an act of aggression; it's an act of liberation. The heart cannot hold both divine love and rival allegiances. To "drive out" false gods is to make room for peace, for compassion, for the indwelling presence that heals and renews.

Jesus echoes this in Luke 11:1–13. He teaches us to pray, "Your kingdom come, your will be done." Every prayer of surrender becomes an act of cleansing, inviting divine reign to displace the idols of fear, pride, and control. Prayer isn't an escape from the struggle; it's participation in it. The Spirit moves through our willingness, tearing down what enslaves and planting new life in its place.

In Christ, this clearing becomes inward and universal. The battle is waged not with weapons but with forgiveness, humility, and love. He enters the land of the human heart, dismantling the idols that blind us and replacing them with grace. Holiness, in the end, isn't about exclusion: it's about freedom.

Guiding Truth: Clear the inner land (remove whatever rivals God's love) so peace can dwell where idols once ruled.

Reflection: What "idols" or rival loves still occupy the inner landscape of my heart? How might prayer and repentance become acts of clearing space for God's peace and presence?

Prayer: Holy One, search me and clear what clings to my soul. Uproot the fears and idols that dull my love. Make my heart your dwelling place (free, open, and whole) so your peace may reign within and through me. Amen.

Day 49: Boundaries, Cities, and the Justice of Mercy

Reading: Numbers 34:1–35:34

As the wilderness journey nears its end, God gives Israel a vision of order: a map for the promised land and instructions for its life together. First come the boundaries of Canaan: a geography drawn not for possession but for stewardship. Then come the forty-eight cities for the Levites, scattered throughout the tribes, anchoring every region with worship, wisdom, and care. And finally come the six cities of refuge, places of sanctuary where those who kill unintentionally can flee for safety until justice is done.

At first, these laws and borders may seem bureaucratic and even dry. But beneath their precision lies a theology of belonging and responsibility. The land is not a prize to seize; it's a gift to receive. Boundaries remind people that creation is not theirs to dominate but to tend. Each tribe is given its portion, but no one owns the promise: God does. The geography of grace requires limits so that justice, community, and rest can flourish.

The Levite cities show another truth: holiness must be dispersed. Worship is not confined to one sanctuary but spread among the people. Every tribe has within it a reminder of God's presence and a center for teaching, counsel, and compassion. In this, God weaves faith into daily geography, embedding it in the neighborhood.

And the cities of refuge reveal divine mercy in a world scarred by violence. These sanctuaries don't erase accountability; they protect dignity while truth is discerned. They embody a balance between justice and grace: between the human impulse to retaliate and the divine call to restore. Even those accused of grave wrong are not beyond the shelter of mercy. In the cities of refuge, we glimpse the heart of God: justice tempered by compassion, law held open by grace.

Spiritually, this passage teaches that holiness has structure. Grace isn't chaos; it has borders that safeguard life and relationships. Love without form can easily become sentimentality, just as law without mercy becomes cruelty. God's vision holds both together: a land ordered for life, a community structured for peace, a justice system infused with mercy.

In Luke 11:1–13, Jesus teaches us to pray, "Forgive us our sins, for we also forgive everyone who sins against us." This is the inner echo of the cities of refuge. Prayer becomes the place of sanctuary where we face our failures and receive pardon. Christ himself becomes the ultimate refuge: our shelter from accusation, the High Priest whose own death frees us from guilt. In him, the boundaries of holiness no longer exclude; they embrace. The land of promise becomes not territory but kingdom, where mercy and truth meet.

For our lives today, this passage calls us to build communities shaped by the same justice of mercy. We need boundaries that protect, presence that blesses, and refuges that heal. To follow Jesus is to embody this divine architecture: ordered love, dispersed holiness, and open-handed compassion.

Guiding Truth: Live within the boundaries of love: build spaces where justice and mercy dwell together, and every soul can find refuge.

Reflection: How can I establish healthy spiritual and relational boundaries that reflect God's justice and care? Where might I be called to create "cities of refuge" in my world: places of forgiveness, fairness, and safety for others?

Prayer: God of justice and mercy, teach me to live within the wide boundaries of your love. Make my life a refuge for others, my community a place of truth and grace. May your order bring peace, and your mercy shape every part of what I build and protect. Amen.

Day 50: The Last Word of the Wilderness

Reading: Numbers 36:1–13

The book of Numbers closes not with a miracle or battle, but with a quiet conversation about inheritance and justice. The daughters of Zelophehad (those same courageous women who once stood before Moses to claim their father's name and portion) appear again. Their story had changed Israel's law so that women could inherit when there were no sons. Now, tribal leaders from Manasseh approach Moses with a concern: if these daughters marry outside their tribe, their inherited land will be transferred to another tribe, disrupting the delicate balance of the Promised Land.

God's response through Moses is practical and tender: the daughters may marry whomever they wish, but within their father's tribe, so the inheritance remains intact. The daughters obey, marrying cousins within Manasseh. It's not a restrictive ending, but a reconciling one: a way of holding justice and communal integrity together. The story ends with order restored, promises honored, and God's people standing at the edge of fulfillment.

This final chapter is deeply symbolic. After all the wandering, rebellion, and mercy, the book concludes with a vision of balance: love and law in harmony, personal freedom within communal responsibility. The daughters of Zelophehad, whose courage once expanded the boundaries of justice, now model humility and faithfulness. They remind us that genuine freedom doesn't reject constraint; it finds grace within it. The inheritance of God's people is always relational.

Spiritually, Numbers 36 invites us to hold together two truths: that God cares for both individual dignity and communal wholeness. We often lean too far one way: either exalting personal freedom at the expense of others, or demanding order that crushes the person. But God's wisdom weaves both together in covenantal faithfulness. The divine intention is not control, but communion: a people free and faithful, diverse yet bound together by love and shared promise.

In Luke 11:1–13, Jesus teaches us to pray, "Your kingdom come." That prayer gathers these same tensions (personal and communal, freedom and obedience, justice and mercy) into one cry of trust. The daughters' story is a living version of that prayer: "May your will be done, even in our inheritance, even in our choices." Their obedience isn't submission to power but participation in the faithfulness that holds community together.

The book ends with these women's names echoing once more: Mahlah, Tirzah, Hoglah, Milcah, and Noah. Their courage and faith bookend the story of the wilderness. What began in loss ends in promise kept. God's covenant proves steady, both flexible and firm. The wilderness is behind them; Canaan lies ahead. The story closes not with triumphal noise, but with faithfulness: the kind that sustains generations.

Guiding Truth: True faith lives in the harmony of freedom and faithfulness: seeking both personal grace and communal good.

Reflection: How can I balance personal freedom with responsibility to others in the way I live and lead? What might it look like to trust God's boundaries as expressions of love rather than limits on joy?

Prayer: Faithful God, teach me the wisdom of balance: freedom that serves, love that honors, obedience that liberates. As I stand on the edge of new seasons, help me carry your justice and mercy together into all I inherit and all I give away. Amen.

Appendix 1: Would You Help?

Writing a book takes immense effort. It's a sustained labor of love over months, even years. Every page carries hours of thought, prayer, revision, and hope. And while the writing may be solitary, the life of a book is communal. That's where you come in. If this book has meant something to you, I'd be deeply grateful if you could help it find its way into more hands and hearts.

There are two simple but powerful ways you can do that.

First, consider leaving a short review on Amazon (and Goodreads would be wonderful too). Even just a few sentences can help others discover the book, as reviews significantly influence how books are recommended and shared online. You can do that by visiting Amazon or searching for this book and writing a review. Even a short note helps people find the book.

Second, if the book has stirred something in you, would you share it with others: friends, groups, churches, or anyone who might benefit from its message?

Your support helps keep this work going, and it means more than I can say. Thank you for being part of this journey.

Find this book on these pages:
1. Amazon:
https://www.amazon.com.au/stores/author/B008NI4ORQ
2. Goodreads:
https://www.goodreads.com/author/show/20347171.Graham_Joseph
_Hill
3. Author Website:

https://grahamjosephhill.com/books/

Appendix 2: About Me

Graham Joseph Hill (OAM, PhD) is an Adjunct Research Fellow and Associate Professor at Charles Sturt University, and one of Australia's most prolific and awarded Christian authors. He's written more than twenty books, including *Salt, Light, and a City*, which was named Jesus Creed's 2012 Book of the Year (church category); *Healing Our Broken Humanity* (with Grace Ji-Sun Kim), named Outreach Magazine's 2019 Resource of the Year (culture category); and *World Christianity*, shortlisted for the 2025 Australian Christian Book of the Year. In 2024, Graham was awarded the Medal of the Order of Australia (OAM) for his service to theological education. He lives in Sydney with his wife, Shyn.

Author and Ministry Websites

GrahamJosephHill.com
GrahamJosephHill.Substack.com
youtube.com/@GrahamJosephHill_Author
Linktr.ee/dailydevotions
facebook.com/grahamjosephhill/
instagram.com/grahamjosephhill/
amazon.com.au/stores/author/B008NI4ORQ
goodreads.com/author/show/20347171.Graham_Joseph_Hill

Books

See all my books at GrahamJosephHill.com/books

Appendix 3: Connect With Me

I'd love to stay connected with you. You can sign up to my Substack, Spirituality and Society with Hilly, where I share new writing, spiritual reflections, and updates on future books. Please find me on Substack: https://grahamjosephhill.substack.com

You can also find my books on my website: https://grahamjosephhill.com/books

You can also connect with me through my Facebook author page: https://www.facebook.com/GrahamJosephHill/